TALK SENSE TO YOURSELF:

The Language of Personal Power

By Chick Moorman
Co-Director
The Institute For Personal Power

Library of Congress Catolog
Card Number: 85-090496

ISBN
0-9616046-0-3

Printed in the United States of America by:

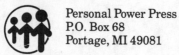

Personal Power Press
P.O. Box 68
Portage, MI 49081

To Yoda, the original Jedi Master;

To my friend, Tim, who helped me learn about mind skills;

To my wife, Dee, who supports me in my quest to become a Jedi Master;

To all the Jedi Knights-In-Training who care about the Force, the power of belief and learning how to manage their own minds;

To all of us who can make it happen.

CONTENTS

Chapter Four

THE LANGUAGE OF POSSIBILITY, 51

Chapter Five

LANGUAGE OF ACCEPTANCE, 80

Chapter Six

THE LANGUAGE OF CONFIDENCE, 114

Chapter Seven

THE LANGUAGE OF HERE AND NOW, 149

Chapter Eight

STRATEGIES FOR CHANGE, 169

PREFACE

This book is about language patterns, the everyday words and phrases you use when you talk to yourself and to others. In it you will learn how to use language to increase your self-esteem, add to your confidence, and greatly increase your sense of personal power.

Language is more than a medium of communication. It is also a medium of perception. The words you choose to use effect how you perceive the world, help create your beliefs, and ultimately influence your actions. In this book you will learn how to purposefully structure your language patterns to create beliefs and actions that leave you in a place you like.

Changing your language can change your life. By learning to view language as programming, you will learn how to program your mind with language that helps you create whatever it is you want from life.

The material for this book is drawn from my own experience as a professional educator and as a person who has chosen to be parent, husband, friend and unique individual. It is an accumulation of words, phrases, and ways of speaking that have worked for me or for others I have observed. It is an effort to share with you what I have come to learn about talking sense to yourself.

My intention is not to create the newest right answer in self-help books, that must be followed to the letter if you desire to experience personal power in your life. Rather, I will provide a smorgasbord of alternatives for you to consider; including suggestions, ideas, strategies, techniques and concepts for you to think about. What you do with these alternatives is up to you. How you choose to fit them to your own best way of living is your choice.

I suggest you read this material and filter it down through your filters. See what makes sense to you. When you find notions that have meaning for you, grab on to them. Put them to use in your life. Let the rest go. Concentrate on those areas that speak to you and integrate them into your style of speaking.

I would like to thank two people who have helped me bring this book to life. My wife, Dee Dishon, has given hours of her time reading the manuscript and making suggestions. Her ideas have improved both the style and content of this book. In addition, her support and encouragement have been consistent and significant.

Sue Dabakey has typed and retyped this material with patience and enthusiasm. Her expertise under pressure has been a valuable contribution to this end result.

I also wish to acknowledge the workshop participants and Michigan State University students who have taken my courses and trainings. Their efforts at putting these ideas to work in their own lives have helped me learn how to present them more effectively.

I have learned and profited immensely from writing this book. Thank you for choosing to let me share it with you.

Chapter One

LANGUAGE AND PERSONAL POWER: AN INTRODUCTION

Personal power begins in your mouth. No, not with the quantity or quality of what you eat. No, not with the number or type of pills you choose or choose not to swallow. No, not even with the variety of decisions you make about cigarettes, dope or drink

While what you choose to take into your system through your lips certainly influences your sense of personal power, it's what passes through your lips in the other direction that counts the most. Yes, personal power starts with your language. It begins with the everyday words you choose to speak to yourself and to others.

There is a powerful theme running throughout this book. It is not difficult to understand nor is it difficult to implement. It is at work in your life right now and will continue to operate regardless of whether or not you are aware of it. The theme is simply this — there is a connection between the words you use, the beliefs you hold, and the actions you take. You can change the quality and direction of your life by purposefully selecting language that will create within you the programming that will get you where you want to be. Yes, by controlling your words you can control your life. Consider the example that follows.

"Makes Me" Language

One of the most commonly used phrases in our culture is "makes me."

"Janet really makes me happy."

"That makes me angry."""

"Children make me nervous."

"Naughty jokes make me feel embarrassed."

"My boss makes me anxious."

"Makes me" is an example of unself-responsible language. That choice of language helps you to see something or someone else as being in control of your responses to life. Every time you use that phrase, you add to your programming that says you are not responsible for your reactions to the people and events in your life. This serves to diminish your sense of personal power.

"Janet makes me happy," is a way of speaking and thinking that gives Janet credit for your joy. It negates your choice of responses in the situation and assigns the responsibility for your happiness to her. If you speak and think in ways that give Janet control of your happiness, you tend to believe you can only be happy around her if she behaves in certain ways. Your degree of happiness is then at the mercy of her behavior.

Similar language can be used to blame others for your miseries. "Janet makes me mad." Now Janet is not only in charge of your happiness, she's also in charge of your unhappiness. If she controls both your happiness and your unhappiness, what is left for you to control?

If your child makes you nervous, then the child is in control of your nervousness. If your boss makes you anxious, then she is in charge of your anxiety. If naughty jokes embarrass you, then joke tellers control your embarrassment. With all those other people and events in control of your responses, it's easy to see why you might have a diminished sense of personal power.

It's a mistake to use language that attributes your happiness, unhappiness, or any other feeling to an external source. Actually, no one can make you feel anything. It's simply not possible for anyone else to create an emotion in you. Emotions are your personal response to an outside act and are within your power to control. Using language that continues the illusion that outside forces create your emotional reactions to life only serves to strengthen your belief that others can "make you."

Do you think sunshine makes you happy? It's not so. Does sunshine make you happy if you are stranded in a boat in the middle of the lake with no shirt to cover your blistering shoulders? Does sunshine cause happiness if you get new skis for Christmas and are waiting for the season's first snowfall? Does sunshine make you happy if you are a farmer and your crops are parching in the field? No, sunshine doesn't make you happy in those cases. And it doesn't make you unhappy, either.

How you choose to interpret the sunshine and how you choose to think about it is what makes you happy or sad, not the sunshine itself. The sun is not in charge of your happiness. You are.

Your boss doesn't make you anxious. You do anxiety to yourself by the thoughts you choose to think or the images you hold in your mind about your boss. Naughty jokes don't embarrass you. You embarrass yourself by the thoughts you choose to think or the pictures you create about naughty jokes. Children don't make you nervous. You again make yourself nervous either by the images you create or the thoughts you think about your children.

It is not your boss, your spouse, your children, or any other external source that causes your emotions. Your feelings are under your control and they begin with the language you use to think about the situations and events of your life.

"He Made Me Do It"

As a fifth-grade teacher, I frequently heard "makes me" language from my students. One of the classic expressions occurred in the middle of an eraser fight. I had been to the office to receive a phone call from a parent. Students were working quietly when I left. I reentered the classroom to find the air filled with erasers. One boy had his arm cocked as I stepped through the doorway. The eraser hurtled through the air and crashed against the wall, just missing another ducking, giggling child.

"Hey!" I interrupted loudly. "What's going on here?"

"He made me do it," responded the eraser launcher.

"Just a minute," I said. "Let me see if I've got this straight. I came in the room. Your arm was cocked. An eraser was in your hand. I watched your hand come forward quickly. The eraser flew across the room. And he *made* you do it?"

"Yes," was the immediate reply.

"Well, I don't get it," I continued. "Say some more."

"Well, he threw one at me," stated the confident ten-year-old, believing that he was now vindicated.

I was never quite sure whether students who used that type of logic were trying to fool me or were fooled themselves. The child who threw the eraser, though, was convinced. He sincerely believed the other child *made him* throw it.

I have had graduate students laugh at that story, immediately sensing an error in the child's logic. "How can anyone make you throw an eraser? That's absurd," they say. Many of those same graduate students, however, held firm beliefs that someone else can make them feel angry or happy. They don't realize their logic is no different than that of the fifth-grade child who believed someone else made him throw the eraser.

We are all in charge of our own responses to the events of our lives. It doesn't matter whether your response is a physical action like slugging another person, pulling a trigger, or jumping off a roof; or if your response is an emotional one such as feeling angry, jealous, or frustrated. No one can make you. Your response is under your jurisdiction. You are responsible for your actions and your feelings.

You may be wondering at this point, "What's all this fuss over 'makes me'? Everyone knows we all control our own emotions. 'Makes me' is simply an idiom and no one takes such usage literally."

Actually, such usage is not only taken literally, it is also taken seriously. Workshop participants who have attended trainings I do in Language and Personal Power have argued long and hard in defense of their belief that someone can make them feel angry or sad. Many people who have taken these language workshops begin by holding firm beliefs that:

- slow drivers can make them frustrated
- icy roads can make them nervous
- people can make them jealous
- weekends can make them happy

- flat tires can make them angry
- other people can make them disgusted, horny, bored, excited, embarrassed, scared, annoyed, and a variety of other emotions

These beliefs that people hold were created and are being reinforced by the programming (words) they choose to use. And the more they hear "makes me" variations on the radio, read it in newspapers, or speak it themselves, the stronger their belief that others can make them becomes.

"Makes Me" Popularity

"Makes me" language abounds in our culture. The programming seems to be everywhere. I hear it on T.V., the radio, and read it in magazines and newspapers. I hear it from co-workers, teachers, children, business people, friends and relatives.

Lyrics of songs are full of "makes me" phraseology.

"Sunshine on my shoulder *makes me* happy, sunshine in my eyes can *make me* cry."

John Denver

"You *make me* feel like a natural woman."

Carol King

"Rainy days and Mondays always *get me* down."

The Carpenters

I believe it's impossible to listen to any radio station for more than 15 minutes without hearing several variations of the "makes me" theme. Imagine what happens to your beliefs after being consistently bombarded with the programming of these "makes me" messages.

Advertisers want us to buy into the "makes me" idea so we will buy their products. We are constantly being conditioned by Madison Avenue to think and speak externally, so we will believe and act (buy) as if their products make us happy.

Yesterday I was informed by a radio announcer that Indian Trails bus service would *"make me* feel right at home." Later that afternoon, I noticed in the newspaper that if I spent $3 to see Dan Aykroyd and Gilda Radner in *It Came From Hollywood* that it would "make me laugh." Still later that night a

T.V. commercial musically told me, "Chevy Chevette, it'll make you happy."

Perhaps you've heard how "You and Betty Crocker can bake (make) someone happy." Or maybe you've learned that Coast soap "will pick you up," or that Texas Instruments "makes learning fun."

Advertisers have a vested interest in us believing that our happiness, health, and excitement come from their products, that their external product can create an emotion (happiness) in us. They want to erode our self-control, our own personal power, and generate in us a dependency on their products. They want us to believe their products can "make us" happy, sexually exciting, and instantly stimulating.

In truth, a Chevy Chevette can no more make me happy than sunshine or another person can. I own a Chevy Chevette and sometimes I'm happy with it and other times I'm not. It certainly didn't make me happy the day the sun visor on the driver's side broke. And it didn't make me unhappy, either. The external object (the Chevette) has no power over my feelings. *I* make me feel, and on that occasion, I chose to feel upset.

From Words To Action

Words of advertisers combine with those spoken by colleagues, friends, and relatives to make up part of your programming. The words you use when you speak to yourself or to others add to it. Given enough repetitions, you develop beliefs that are consistent with the programming you receive.

Seen in this perspective, "makes me" becomes much more than just a harmless conversational pattern. It becomes programming that influences both the beliefs you hold and the action you take as a result of those beliefs. It works like this.

Words structure your thoughts. If you use "makes me" phraseology, your thoughts reflect that choice of words and become, "She made me do it," or "He made me nervous." Repeated often enough, you begin to believe, like some participants who attend my workshops, that others can *make you* feel and act in certain ways.

Using words to program your mind is like wearing grooves on a record. The more you think "makes me" thoughts, the deeper the impression becomes on your mind and the more you believe others can make you. Eventually, you internalize a belief in powerlessness and other-directedness.

Once belief is firmly established in your mind, behavior consistent with your belief follows. If you strongly believe that others can make you react, you will exhibit one set of behaviors. If you believe others do not make you react, you do a different set of behaviors.

If your beliefs are that people can indeed make you respond at a feeling level, you may stay away from an individual because you think he has the power to make you nervous. You might buy something from the salesperson so he doesn't make you feel cheap. You will go to the party instead of staying home so the host doesn't make you feel guilty.

If your belief is that *you* are in charge of your emotions, you act in ways that reflect that belief. If you choose to stay away from certain people, your choice flows from preference and not because someone can make you feel nervous. You turn down the salesman because you know it's *you* who decides whether or not to feel cheap. You choose not to go to the party and decide for yourself whether you want to feel guilty or not.

"Makes me" is much more than just an innocent phrase. It is input you use to program your marvelous bio-computer (mind). It is programming that eventually results in beliefs which influence your actions, which determine in large measure the quality of your living. Think about it.

"Makes me" language flows two ways. You can speak as if others control you (She made me mad). Or you can speak as if you control others (I make her nervous). Examples of language that helps create the illusion that you are in charge of others' emotional responses follow.

"I hurt her feelings."
"I wounded his pride."
"I hope this doesn't make him mad."
"I caused her lots of embarrassment."
"I certainly upset his equilibrium."

A danger in speaking as if you control others' reactions is you start believing you have some control over their responses. When you believe you are in charge of another person's emotional responses, you act in ways consistent with that belief. You act as a shock absorber and refrain from saying certain

7

things because it might make someone mad. You don't tell your spouse you met an old friend today because it might make her jealous. You say you like the present even though you know you'll never wear it, so you won't hurt her feelings.

When you believe others control their own emotional responses, you behave in ways that demonstrate that belief. You tell your spouse about your meeting and experience her emotional reaction as belonging to her. You return the present, and let the giver choose his own emotional response. You behave less as a shock absorber and allow people to respond from their interpretation of the event. You become more honest and share your feelings more often.

Regardless of whether your actions are to return the present or keep it hanging in the closet, go to the party or stay home, your action flows out of your beliefs. And those beliefs begin with language, the everyday words you use to talk to yourself and others.

The connection between the words you use and the behaviors you exhibit in your life is shown on the following schematic drawing.

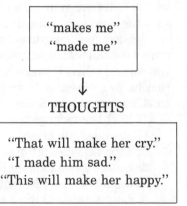

Words are the beginning of how you structure your life. They are your programming.

The words you use structure your thoughts.

WORDS

"makes me"
"made me"

↓

THOUGHTS

"That will make her cry."
"I made him sad."
"This will make her happy."

↓

BELIEFS

Repetitive thought turns into belief.	"What I do controls her response." "What she does controls my response."

↓

ACTION

Your behavior flows out of your belief.	silence buy an unwanted product go to the party

By following this diagram, you can see that words are the tools which eventually shape your actions. The words you use form the thoughts you think. The thoughts you think turn into the beliefs you hold. The beliefs you hold influence your behavior. The behaviors you exhibit define and direct your living.

Words are the beginning of how you structure your life. In terms of self-responsibility and personal power, it works like this: self-responsible behavior flows out of self-responsible beliefs; self-responsible beliefs are generated by self-responsible thoughts; self-responsible thoughts are created with self-responsible language.

To move toward more self-responsible behavior and toward a greater sense of personal power in your life, you can begin by reprogramming your mind using self-responsible words. Yes, to change the direction and outcome of your life, you can begin by changing your words.

Changing Your Language

Why not increase your own sense of personal power by using a style of language that helps you see yourself as the source of your reactions and others as the source of their reactions? Why not choose words and phrases that leave you in control of you and allow others to control themselves? Why not eliminate "makes me" phraseology and choose language patterns that strengthen your belief in yourself and your ability to be in charge of your own response?

To change your language, it is necessary to pay attention to your words so that you become aware of the language you do use. Before you can move from what is to something else, it is important to become aware of what is.

Awareness is essential. If I'm standing on your foot while we're having a conversation and I don't know it, there's nothing I can do about it. I won't move my foot unless I become aware of the situation. Once you tell me, "Hey, you're standing on my foot," I alter my awareness and can then figure out an appropriate response.

To heighten your awareness, listen for examples of "makes me" phrases this week. Keep a "makes me" journal. Monitor where you hear those phrases. Are they on T.V., in the music you listen to, or contained in the newspapers and magazines you read? Are they originating from you or coming from others? Is there some person in your life who uses "makes me" language frequently? Are there people or situations that exist in your life where *you* are more likely to activate that style of language?

My hunch is that you'll be hearing more "makes me" talk this week, probably more than you imagine. Just reading this chapter will heighten your awareness and help you to notice it. Keep track. It's a way to help you focus on your own language patterns and the first step toward change.

"I Make Me"

One effective way of changing "makes me" language is to change the word that immediately precedes "makes me" to "I." "Sad movies make me cry" then becomes "I make me cry." "Naughty jokes make me feel embarrassed" is changed to "I make me feel embarrassed." "You turn me on" becomes "I turn me on."

Using "I" in front of "makes me" puts you in charge. That technique helps keep your consciousness focused on the real power you have. It's a visible and audible reminder that you are in control, that you are responsible, that it's you who owns your feelings and other responses.

Putting "I" before "makes me" may sound awkward at first. "I made myself angry," "I make me frustrated," and "I made myself jealous" are certainly not common phrases. Not many people talk that way.

"I made myself angry" sounds strange because you're not used to hearing and thinking in those terms. Use "I make me" phraseology for awhile. Persist and you will learn to feel increasingly comfortable with it.

I'm Choosing"

Another way of speaking that leaves you clearly in control of your responses is to use the phrase "I'm choosing." Examples follow:

"I'm choosing to be mad."

"I chose embarrassment when he said that."

"Right now I'm choosing anger."

By using the words "I'm choosing," you remind yourself of the role you play in activating your emotional responses. You bring your choice in the situation to a conscious level. Once you are consciously aware of your choice, you've increased your options and your sense of personal power.

Reporting Feelings

Another alternative is that of simply stating your feelings. For instance, I bought my daughter a $35 baseball glove and two days later she left it out in the rain. When I saw the glove soaked and getting wetter, I chose to get angry. I immediately shared my anger with her.

I didn't say "You make me so angry!" or even, "It makes me angry to see your glove in the rain!" I simply described the situation and stated my feelings, "I'm angry!" I then went on to explain that baseball gloves were not for leaving in the rain.

It's important to make the distinction that the glove or my daughter didn't make me angry. I chose to be angry. It was a decision I made and a feeling I activated. I own it. It's mine. Therefore, I want to use words that remind me that I'm in charge of my anger and that I am the one who activates it.

"I'm feeling sad," "I'm frustrated," and "I feel excited," are ways to express your emotions without communicating that someone "makes you." By simply reporting your feelings, you are owning them. They become yours. Your response comes from within and is more self-responsible.

When you state your feelings without the "makes me" addition, you are choosing a style of communication that leaves *you* in charge of *you.* The result is more personal power and more control. And it all begins with your choice of words.

By purposefully changing "makes me" phraseology to "I make me," "I'm choosing to be," "I feel . . . ," you will begin to internally challenge the notion that others can make you feel or act in certain ways. By becoming increasingly aware of this language pattern and by consciously changing it, you will begin to develop new beliefs. In time, by using the new words to reprogram your mind, you will exhibit new self-responsible behavior in line with those beliefs.

Other "Makes Me" Variations

As your skill in noticing and rephrasing "makes me" language increases and your self-responsible behaviors expand, you will begin to detect new, more subtle variations on the "makes me" theme. "Makes me" language comes in a variety of shapes, forms and intensities, not always recognized quickly. Some of them follow:

"It's frustrating me."
"You're embarrassing me."
"Heights scare me."
"He offends me."
"She bothers me."
"He let me down."
"You disappoint me."
"That annoys me."
"That's depressing."

Each of these sentences is "makes me" in disguise. Each is an example of language that diminishes your personal power and leaves someone or something else in control of your response. Each is programming that helps you believe you are not responsible for your feelings. Let's take a closer look.

"It's frustrating me."

It doesn't frustrate me. Whatever *it* is, *it* doesn't have the power to frustrate me. I can only do frustration to myself. I create my own frustration by the thoughts I choose to think, and by how I choose to interpret *it*.

"You're embarrassing me."

You don't embarrass me. No one can embarrass me without my own consent. If I'm embarrassed, it's because I've bought into the idea.

"Heights scare me."

Heights scare me? Do you suppose heights sneak up behind me and say "Boo!"? No, heights are just heights. They have no power to scare anyone. I scare me.

If I think, "I'm going to fall," or "I could get killed," I will scare myself with those thoughts. If I hold an image in my mind of being carried off to the hospital, I will scare myself with that image. If I activate previous programming in the form of a belief I hold, "Heights are dangerous," I scare myself with that belief. Regardless of whether I think the thought, hold the image, or activate the belief, I am the one who scares me. The height doesn't do it. I do it to myself.

"He offends me."

People don't offend or annoy me. I can only do that myself. Being offended or being annoyed is my reaction and within my power to control. It is my unique personal response to another person and I am in charge of that, not them.

Take person X for example. Some people get scared around person X. Some are happy. Others do nervousness. Some people even get sexually excited and have noticeable physical reactions around the person. Others get sick in her presence.

We all react differently to person X. Is person X responsible for each of our reactions? Did she make us all react those ways? Of course not. We are responsible for our own reactions.

We react differently to person X because we make different interpretations about her. We see her through different eyes, different beliefs, and different life experiences.

"She bothers me."

She doesn't bother me. I bother myself by the interpretations I attach to what she does. In fact, she may even be consciously trying to bother me. Yet, if I'm preoccupied with thoughts about love, or seeing her behavior as not related to me in any way, I'm not bothered. I'm the only one who can bother me.

"He let me down."

If he can let me down then he must be in control of me. My choice of language here reflects a belief that he is in charge of my up/down buttons. When I believe he can let me down, then his actions determine whether or not I am up or down. I have given him the power to affect my up or down-ness

"You disappoint me."

Just as being up and down is really under my control, so is disappointment. No one has the power to disappoint me. I cause myself to be disappointed.

"He let me down," or "You disappoint me," are clues that I've been living vicariously through others. They are a sign that I've been holding expectations that I want someone else to satisfy. If the other person doesn't deliver and satisfy my desires and I choose words that blame him, I in effect prevent myself from taking a look at why I'm living through him in the first place.

I won't feel let down or disappointed unless I've been leaning on someone. That choice of words is a clue that I've been leaning and is a signal of my dependency. (The relationship between dependency and personal power will be discussed later in Chapter Four.)

"That annoys me."

That doesn't annoy me. *That* doesn't have the power to annoy me. I annoy me by the way I think about and interpret the situation or by the previous programming I activate. And I'll stay annoyed for as long as I choose to hold on to those thoughts, that interpretation or run the old programming.

14

Look Inward

Believing, thinking, and speaking in language like, "That annoys me," or "She offends me," is a waste of time and energy. It effectively prevents me from spending any effort examining what it is that's in me that reacts to the person that way. It keeps me focusing outward, away from myself to someone or something I have little or no control over.

Far better to focus inward. When I hear myself saying, "What a boring class," it's more helpful to ask, "Why am I choosing to bore myself?" than it is to continue to believe the class bores me. When I notice my self-talk is, "She bothers me," I get more benefit from asking myself, "What am I activating within me that will not accept her imperfections?" rather than holding on to the misconception that she controls my reaction. When I notice my thoughts contain language like "He annoys me," I get more useful results pondering, "Why am I giving him the power to annoy me?" than I do from, "Why is he doing this to me?"

When you notice your reaction is boredom, annoyance, anxiety, depression, joy, excitement, arousal, or any other emotion, look inward for explanations and meaning. That's where the power originates. That's where the answers are. Even if you don't find answers to your questions, asking them will help you remind yourself that it's you that controls your reactions. You will then be more likely to choose a reaction that leaves you in a place you like or create one that leaves you feeling powerful and in control.

"That's Depressing"

Nothing is depressing unless you think it's depressing. There is *no* situation, event, or person that is depressing to everyone. There are only people and events that some of us interpret as depressing.

Depression is not a thing. It is a process that you engage in, something you do to yourself. Use words that help you see depression as a process. Choose language that brings to your conscious attention the part you play in that process.

Replace "That's depressing" with "I'm doing depression" or "I am depressing."

When you say, "I'm doing depression," you take responsibility for your depression. That phraseology will help you hear the choice you have in maintaining its existence.

By talking about your situation as something you do (I'm doing anxiety right now), you remind yourself that anxiety is within your power to generate. And if you believe you generate it, you are in a better position to control it.

When I choose irritation, I talk to myself exactly like that. I say, "I'm choosing irritation now," or "I'm doing irritation." My next remark to myself is usually, "Now why would I want to do that?" Once I ask myself that question, I'm well on my way to choosing some other feeling.

Irritation, depression, anxiety, frustration and other emotional reactions are not something you get. They are something you do. Use language that helps you understand that relationship and you will increase your sense of personal power.

More "Makes Me"

Still other variations of the "makes me" phrase follow:
"That's tying me up in knots."
"Young children wear me down."
"You threw me with that one."
"You put me down yesterday."
"He steered me wrong."
"He put me on the spot."
"That rubs me the wrong way."
"My car just can't go by there without stopping."
"He changed my mind."
"She got me going."
"It irks me."
"You lost me completely."
"She gave me a complex."

In each case above, the statement is an attempt to shift responsibility for the feeling or reaction from the speaker to someone or something else. Shifting that responsibility may feel good for the moment, because if you can get yourself to believe you are not responsible for something, then you don't have to do anything about it. You can just blame others (it or they), and feel smug and content knowing it's not your fault.

After all, someone else made you.

While you may gain short term, you lose in the long run. You lose because every time you use "makes me" language, you reinforce the notion that you're not in control. After many repetitions of that style of language, you begin to act as if others can make you. You can believe that your reactions are caused by others if you want to. However, you pay a price in lost power and self-responsibility when you lead a life based on the false notion that others can control you so easily.

Do you really want to give others the power to tie you up in knots? Do you really think it's helpful to believe small children wear you down? Is there some advantage in believing others can put you on the spot?

"Makes Me" And The Sex Connection

Verbal interactions between sexual partners are full of "makes me" variations. Consider the following phraseology:
"You turn me on."
"You excite me."
"You light my fire."
"She turned my head."
"He keeps me hanging on."
"She keeps stringing me along."
"He broke my heart."
"He swept me off my feet."

Each of these is another attempt to activate the "makes me" theme. Each is giving the other person credit for your feeling or reaction. Each is simply not true.

No one can turn you on. What really happens is you turn yourself on. You excite yourself by the thoughts you choose to think about another person. If you choose not to think erotic, sexy thoughts about the person, you don't turn yourself on. If you think erotic, sexy thoughts, you excite yourself with them. And the other person doesn't even have to be present for you to do it. This technique is used all the time, and it even has a special name. It's called a fantasy.

If the other person turned you on, then you would be on every time that person was around you, or at least every time that person wanted you to be on. It doesn't work that way. When that person is around, sometimes you're on and sometimes you're off. In fact, sometimes you're off when the other person wants you to be on and vice versa.

No one lights your fire. You do. You keep you hanging on. You turn your head and you break your own heart. There is no way another person can do any of those things to you. You do them to yourself.

"Makes Me" As Manipulation

There are other people in our lives who would like us to believe the "makes me" myth. They want us to believe it so they can control us. Is there someone in your life who wants you to believe that you will hurt people's feelings if you don't visit on Thanksgiving? Is there someone who wants you to believe you will make him unhappy if you don't make love to him tonight? Is there someone who wants you to believe you will make her happy if you let her use the new car? Beware of people who attempt to lay the "makes me" theme on you. It could be an effort to manipulate.

Also, listen for your own "makes me" language. Manipulation can flow both ways. Believing she can make me feel guilty is no different than believing I can make her feel guilty. It's the same basic notion.

In order for you to get free of "makes me" beliefs and behave in more self-responsible ways yourself, it is necessary to learn to speak with language that leaves you in charge of your responses. It is also necessary to learn to speak with language that communicates others are in charge of their responses.

Learning to use language that leaves you in charge of your responses will help you let others take the responsibility for their responses. And using language that communicates that others are in charge of their responses will help you take responsibility for yours. In each case, responsibility begins with controlling your language.

Summary

I have spent most of this chapter concentrating on one phrase, "makes me" and describing the relationships between the words we speak and the quality of our lives. You may be wondering why all the fuss over one phrase. Can simply changing one phrase really change your life?

There is no single word, idea, phrase, or strategy in this book that alone will dramatically change your life. There is, however, a series of words, phrases, and ways of speaking that, if used collectively and practiced regularly, will develop into a style of communication that will help you change your way of thinking, seeing, believing, and acting.

"Makes me" is only the first of many ways you can change your language to change your life. In the chapters that follow, I will explode the myth that "talk is cheap" and detail ways you use language to rob yourself of joy, harmony, well being, self-esteem, love, and an active sense of personal power. Welcome to the journey.

Chapter Two

WHY LANGUAGE IS IMPORTANT

"Don't tell me, show me."

"Actions speak louder than words."

"Be a doer, not a talker."

The above statements are variations of "talk is cheap." They explain a view of personal growth that suggests it takes action to move forward, not words. The sentences are intended to make the point that talking about change is not enough, that deliberate action is necessary for it to occur.

I do not quarrel with the concept that action is necessary to produce change. I endorse it. I would like to suggest, however, that choosing words is an action. Speaking words is an action. And thinking about the words you have just spoken is also an action. Deliberately choosing specific words, purposefully constructing language patterns, and speaking in that chosen style is not only action, it is some of the most meaningful action you can take if change or personal growth is your goal.

When you take direct action by using new words, as detailed in the chapters that follow, you will notice that you will begin to think differently about yourself and others. You will notice your behavior change and become more consistent with your new language. When you purposefully choose and use new verbal programming, you will slowly change your

20

actions and yourself to fit your new language patterns. Then you will notice the power inherent in language and you will understand that talk is *not* cheap, it *is* expensive!

Mind Power

The mind, more than anything else, determines the quality of your living. Your mind is the central agent in determining whether you experience success or failure, joy or sorrow, sickness or health. Your mind determines whether or not you win or lose, persevere or give up, experience fear or faith.

Your life is an extension of what's in your mind, and whatever you hold there sooner or later materializes. If your mind is filled with self-doubt and self-limiting beliefs, you will create a life of stagnation and failure for yourself. If your mind is filled with confidence and thoughts of unlimited success, you will create a life of joy and success.

If your mind dwells on happiness you produce happiness. If your mind is filled with beliefs about lack and limitation then you produce that for yourself. Your mind creates your reality. It is that important.

Words Make Minds

You can choose your destiny by managing your mind. You are the writer, the director and computer programmer for your own mind, and words are your primary programming tool.

If you use angry words you create an angry mind. If you use happy words, you create a happy mind. If your words are filled with worry, so is your mind. If your words are filled with peace, then your mind is programmed to take on that condition.

Words make minds and in turn create your reality. If your mind is programmed with helpful, useful words, it will create helpful, useful results for you. If it is filled with harmful words, it will create inadequate, harmful results.

How your mind functions on any given day depends on the words it has to work with. Words are tools. They limit or free, caution or motivate, energize or drain. They produce misery or cause happiness, produce abundance or cause lack. Words are tools and like any tools they can be used to build or destroy.

The words you use and the thoughts you think also behave like seeds you plant in your mind. They take root, sprout quickly and grow strong. And if those words and thoughts are repeated often enough they grow into beliefs.

If your words are consistently those of self-limitation (can't, never, impossible), you develop self-limiting beliefs. If you repeatedly use words that nourish (can, of course, possible), you develop beliefs about yourself as worthwhile and limitless.

Words behave like hypnotic forces. Whether talking to others or talking to yourself, your communication acts like the constant repetition of a hypnotist. Your beliefs are reinforced constantly by the words you choose to use. And as you continue the process of self-hypnosis by using the same words over and over, your beliefs become stronger.

All your language makes an impression on your subconscious mind. Think of each word in terms of a checkmark. Enough marks and you fill a page. Enough pages and you create a book. Enough books and you've got a library.

What currently exists in the library of your subconscious mind? What words are contained there? Are they positive or negative? Restrictive or freeing? Healthful or sickly? What beliefs exist in the library of your mind?

Beliefs to Action

Beliefs are important because action flows out of belief. If you believe you are unworthy, you act unworthy. If you believe you are a leader, you act like a leader. If you believe you are a valuable member of our team, you act like a valuable member of our team. Each of us, all day long, is in the process of acting out our beliefs. And through our beliefs, our minds convert words into being.

In my work as a classroom teacher and teacher consultant, I have witnessed this phenomenon many times. Children who believe they can read, act like they can read. Children who believe they are troublemakers, make trouble. Children who believe they have something to offer, end up offering something. Children who have positive, healthy beliefs about themselves are easy to work with. They act friendly, self-responsible and are generally happy. They act confident, assume they will succeed, and eventually do.

On the other hand, it is a different kind of challenge to work with children who believe they are not able, capable or worthwhile. Their actions match their beliefs regardless of whether or not their beliefs are accurate. Children who believe they are not artistic, act unartistic. Children who believe they are unintelligent, act unintelligent. It matters less whether they are unartistic or unintelligent. It matters more whether or not they believe they are.

We Prove Our Beliefs To Ourselves

Beliefs eventually become reality because we constantly engage in proving our beliefs to ourselves. If you believe you are clumsy, you prove that to yourself by noticing the times you do something that fits with your belief. Because you have a lot of time and energy invested in creating that belief, you are more likely to notice your clumsy acts. You dwell on your clumsiness, think about it, remind yourself of it, and tell others about it. Your graceful acts go unnoticed or you pay only slight attention to them. In that way, over time, you prove your clumsiness to yourself. That in turn strengthens your belief in your own clumsiness and gives you even more to prove the next time.

Words As Power

We have a fundamental language choice in our lives. We can choose our own words or use the programming that is predominate in our culture. We can intentionally select words to fit our purposes or use what we've learned from radio, newspapers, friends and relatives.

Most of us, without giving much thought to it, use the words that are popular in our society. Few of us choose words consciously to produce a desired result. Few of us see words as programming and use them as a delivery system to get us to a specific destination. Few of us intentionally use words that leave us in a place we like.

When you take control of the words you use and choose them purposefully, you take control of your life. You become more self-developed and less at the mercy of culturation and outside influences. You become better able to work the controls of your life and get where you want to go. You are in charge. You have a greater degree of personal power.

To Be Able

Be careful not to misinterpret here. I'm not talking about power in the sense of power-crazed, power-hungry, power-starved, or power-mad. Nor am I talking about power over others, either overt or subtle.

I am advocating using words that help you to become power-full in line with the definition of power that comes from the Latin, *potere,* which means "to be able." I advocate that we all learn to see ourselves as able — to control our own lives and shape our own destinies; able to choose goals and determine ways to get there; able to decide what's best for us and then act on those choices.

One way you can increase your personal power through language is to think of words as feedback. Your words serve as a constant source of information concerning what you've been thinking, imagining, and believing. By paying attention to and monitoring your words, you can glean valuable clues as to the direction your life is headed. Notice the words you use. There are messages there for you. Listen to your self-talk. You are telling yourself something while you're telling yourself something.

Language usually points towards or away from something. By examining the direction of your words, you can determine the direction of your life. Once you are in touch with that direction, you are in a position to change it if you choose.

If you notice your language is filled with words of self-doubt, be assured that over time you will develop beliefs that are consistent with your words. Your actions will flow from those beliefs and you'll activate behaviors that are congruent with them. Your actions will be tentative. You will make decisions slowly and change your mind often. You'll procrastinate. You'll seek advice from others, follow it, and worry about your decisions. Your unconfident actions will reinforce your original words of self-doubt and your doubt will grow stronger.

You can change your unconfident acts by changing your words. You have the power to speak with the language of confidence (see Chapter Six). By using confident words, you'll think

24

confident thoughts, develop confident beliefs, and in turn act confidently. Now your actions will be steady and assured. You'll make decisions quickly and rarely change your mind. You'll take action now. If you seek advice from others, you'll use it to make your own decisions. Once you decide, you won't worry. You'll move on to reinforce your belief in yourself as a confident person and your confidence will grow stronger.

Your words and language also serve as a feedback as to what you've been pretending and imagining in your life. We are all busy pretending certain things about ourselves and one another. Many times our pretending is so real we don't even admit to ourselves we are pretending. We simply say. "That's just the way I am," or "That's the way things are."

Have you been pretending to be creative or uncreative? Do you pretend to be disorganized or organized? Do you pretend to be tired or full of energy? Listen to your words. There are clues there for you to help you determine what it is you've been pretending.

Monitoring your language is also important feedback for determining what it is you imagine. Do you imagine you're a likeable person or unlikeable? Do you hold images of yourself as worthy or unworthy? Do you see yourself as living in lack or living in abundance?

Images are important because you become what you imagine yourself to be. If you hold images of yourself as healthy and full of energy, there's a greater likelihood you will be healthy and full of energy. If you don't imagine yourself becoming prosperous, chances are it won't happen for you.

As you learn to become increasingly conscious of your words, you can tune into the information they provide about the images you've been creating. Once you become aware of your images, you can change them if you choose.

Words As Opportunity

Your words are an opportunity. They are an opportunity to examine what you are really telling yourself. They are an opportunity to take firmer control of your life and move in directions that are satisfying, meaningful, and uplifting. They are an opportunity to increase your sense of personal power.

To take advantage of those opportunities, it is necessary to become aware of your language. Just being slightly more

25

aware of your language can alter how you speak, think, and believe. Without awareness of your words and the results they produce, you are powerless to change them. With awareness you have choice.

Become conscious of your words as you read the remaining chapters in this book. Do the exercises that ask you to monitor your language. Pay close attention to your style of speaking to yourself and to others.

Listen to your words. You may hear potential danger there, or you may find the source of your strength. You may discover how you limit or how you free yourself. You may hear words you use to propel yourself into action or find language you use to postpone.

Summary

There is personal power in choosing language. And it's a healthy liberating power that leads to self-responsibility and self-direction. As you learn to choose your own words and design your own talk, you will come to hear and view yourself as a person with the capacity to manage your own mind. As you continue to choose words on purpose, you will continue to reinforce your belief in your ability of self-direction.

Your words create thought. Your thoughts create belief. Your beliefs influence action. In this way, your life eventually becomes congruent with your words. This is how you create your own reality.

When you decide to take charge of your words, you decide to take charge of your life. By carefully choosing the words you use, you program your own mind and in turn change your life.

Remember, your words are not cheap. They are expensive.

Chapter Three

THE LANGUAGE OF
SELF-RESPONSIBILITY

What's your self-responsibility quotient? To what degree do you believe you control your own life? How are you at taking responsibility for the circumstances, events, and situations that exist for you right now? Want to find out? Your language offers you clues. Examine it closely and you can learn valuable lessons about yourself.

Read through the following sentences. Make a check mark in front of the ones you've heard yourself say. Place an X in front of the ones that you feel are examples of self-responsible language. Do it now.

1. I have to get going now.
2. I need a ride downtown.
3. It's cold in here.
4. We don't like that kind of behavior.
5. The pressure got to him.
6. When the mood overtakes me, I get really excited.
7. I'm very fortunate to have met her.

How many did you X as examples of self-responsible language? Actually, none of the sentences above contains self-responsible language or reflects a self-responsible way of looking at the world. Each contains unself-responsible phrases and each indicates one way you are giving up personal power by not assuming control in your life. Let's take a closer look.

THE LANGUAGE OF LUCK

There are many words and phrases in our language that refer to the concept of luck. Some of the more popular words are good fortune, chance, magic, and coincidence. These words, which embellish the myth that luck exists and is at work in our lives, can be heard in sentences like the following:

"I really *lucked* out."

"She led a *charmed* life."

"Wow, what a *coincidence!*"

"What an *unfortunate* string of events."

"I'm just *jinxed* today."

A more personal example occurred during the writing of *Our Classroom: We Can Learn Together,* which I wrote with my wife, Dee Dishon. We completed three chapters and an outline and mailed them to Prentice-Hall. When a contract was offered to us several weeks later, we chose to be delighted. We realized that only a small percentage of books sent unsolicited through the mail ever get past the editor's desk, much less get accepted for publication.

When I shared our success with a friend of mine and told him about the odds of our book being accepted, he replied, "Boy, were you lucky!" I just smiled because his words told more about him than they did about us or our book.

Acceptance of the *Our Classroom* book had nothing to do with luck. It had to do with five years of collecting material and three years of writing during evenings and on weekends. It had to do with our teaching the material to others and learning it thoroughly. It had to do with *US*: our skills, our beliefs, and our persistence.

I feel powerful knowing I helped write that book. I feel satisfaction knowing someone else recognized our ideas as useful. I feel confident, self-reliant, and in control knowing I was a part of that successful effort. Now, why would I want to assign those positive feelings to some unknown, nebulous force termed Luck? Why would I want to give up ownership of all that effort and assign it instead to good fortune? And why would I want to see myself as the recipient of something that just came my way? The answer to each question is, I don't.

I want to use words that give me the credit I deserve. I want to choose a style of language that reinforces my belief that I am in control of my life events and the situations that surround me. I want to use phrases that leave me in charge.

It wasn't long after that incident with our book that one of my graduate students remarked, "How fortunate you are to have a wife who understands you, who listens, and who shares your beliefs." Fortunate? Now even my taste in women is attributed to luck! Hardly.

Who do you think is responsible for picking my wife, anyway? I am. I picked her from all the women I've known in my life. She's the one I want to live with and love with more than anyone else I know.

It certainly isn't circumstance or magic that creates our mutual understanding or our ability to listen to each other. It is work, effort, and our belief that the work and effort are worth it. We work at creating it the way we like it. We don't leave it to chance.

I suppose you could also say I'm lucky she wants me! Now why would I want to think that? I prefer to think she wants me because of me. I'm positive, caring, sexy, funny, helpful, and modest. I want to give myself some credit for being likeable, desirable, and wanted. The language of luck doesn't help me do that.

Assigning our book's success, our effective relationship, or any other situation in our lives to luck is a way of disowning the role we play in that success or lack of success. It's one more technique for giving up responsibility and giving it to something else, in this case to luck.

The language of luck diminishes personal power. It dilutes the faith and confidence you have in yourself and gives some unknown outside force credit for success and failure. It's a way you have of seeing yourself as helpless, at the mercy of fate or fortune.

Use of the language of luck is a variation on the Blame Game. It sets up a mysterious external force as a source to blame when things don't turn out well.

"I didn't have any luck with him at all."

"Unfortunately, everything went wrong with my presentation."

"It just wasn't in the cards."

I can understand wanting to assign responsibility to fate or fortune when things don't go well. What's harder to understand is when I hear someone give the credit for their hard work and resulting success to the concept of luck.

"I just fell into it."

"I stumbled onto that idea at the library."

"It came my way one day when I was thinking."

"I was just in the right place at the right time."

Maybe there is no such thing as luck. Life appears, in one sense, to be an ongoing mixture of good breaks and bad breaks. Yet in another sense it is really nothing more than good or poor preparation, abundance or lack of skills, seeing many or few alternatives. Opportunities come and opportunities go. How a person chooses to see those opportunities, and the skills and preparation a person brings to those opportunities have more to do with success than good fortune does.

Is it a case of misfortune striking if a person is laid off from a job she held for ten years? A bad break, you say? And what if that person sees the job loss as an opportunity, goes into business for herself, and turns it into a financial success? Now does that make loss of the original job good luck? Perhaps we create our own luck.

I sat in the stands one spring in Payne Park in Sarasota, Florida, where the Chicago White Sox train and watched a coach hit over 200 ground balls to Alan Bannister. From his position at shortstop, Alan would field the ball, throw to first, and return to his position. After an hour and a half of repeating this sequence he trotted off the field soaked in sweat. When he got close to the stands, I asked him why he worked so hard. His response is etched in my memory. He said, "The harder you work, the luckier you get."

Alan Bannister didn't believe in luck. What about you? Where are your beliefs regarding this issue? Your words will give you a clue. Do you hear yourself using "fortunate," "magic," "accidental," "coincidence," and "lucky?" If so, you're using the language of luck to think thoughts that help form and reinforce belief in luck and decrease belief in yourself.

Why not give yourself credit for having the good sense to be in the right place at the right time? How about using words to acknowledge that someone else may have worked harder to get the job or had more skills than you did? Why not choose language to pat yourself on the back after a personal record-breaking 10,000 meter run rather than assigning it to coincidence? You can assign responsibility to luck or you can take it on yourself. Where do you want to place the responsibility?

EXTERNAL SOURCES

Luck is only one of several external sources that can be used to disown personal responsibility for the circumstances of your life. Our language provides a range of alternatives from which to choose if we're interested in side-stepping responsibility and giving up personal power. You may recognize some of the examples that follow.

"I got carried away."

This is a convenient and simple way to begin if you want to fool yourself into believing you are not responsible. After all, how could it possibly be your fault or any of your doing when you were picked up and moved by some obscure, unnamed, external force? The next time you want to disown responsibility for one of your actions, just tell yourself you got carried away. That will alleviate your concern and help you see yourself as unresponsible.

"It just came over me."

This one is a classic. It is an attempt to convey that *"it"* is responsible for your reactions. You can't be held accountable because you were doing fine, rolling along, minding your own business. Then *"it"* came along and came over you. If *"it"* hadn't come over you, everything would have worked out fine. What a shame that *"it"* came over you and forced you to take money from the cash register.

"I don't know what came over me."

This sentence carries unself-responsibility to a new level. Now, not only did *"it"* come over you, but you don't even know what *"it"* is. How can you possibly be responsible for something you can't even explain? Some secret force, which you know nothing about, came over you. Otherwise you never would have called her a dumb bitch.

"Time just got away from me."

If you want to dodge responsibility for being late, this sentence is appropriate. It's intended to give the impression that

31

you were working hard trying not to let time get away, yet despite your valiant efforts, it managed to get away anyhow. What better explanation for showing up five hours late than to blame it on "time getting away."

"I got her at the right time."
or
"I got her at the wrong time."

If you're interested in keeping the responsibility for success or failure in your life off of your own shoulders and avoiding an examination of what you might have contributed to that success or failure, timing is a useful scapegoat. Timing will take either the credit or blame for what happens to you.

For example, it couldn't have been your preparation, presentation, or the two hours sleep you had the night before that resulted in your missing the sale. It was just bad timing.

It wasn't your appearance, your love-making skills, or the fact that you have $500,000.00 in the bank that influenced her to accept your proposal of marriage. Obviously, you just caught her at a good time.

"I didn't have time to write that up."

This is another way to use time to see yourself as not being in control. Responsibility can be uncomfortable. To reduce that discomfort, it is possible to use language patterns to create a view of your world as one in which you have fewer choices. You can use language to help yourself believe that what happens to you is mostly a result of pressures beyond your control.

An alternative to "I didn't have time," is "I didn't take time to write that up." In this case your language helps you create a view of your world as one in which you have more choices. Your language patterns help you focus on the choices you made, the priorities you set, and the responsibility you have.

"It was one of those things."

If it was one of *those* things, no wonder you bombed out. It couldn't be you, your effort, or your attitude that influenced the outcome. It was one of *those* things. Why is it we seldom ask ourselves, "One of *what* things?"

"Thank goodness he hit that home run!"
or
"Thank goodness I got here on time!"

Why thank goodness? What did goodness have to do with it anyway? Did goodness hit the home run? Was goodness responsible that you got there on time? Why not thank the person who hit the home run? He did it, not some invisible controller named Goodness. Why not thank yourself for being here on time. *Goodness* didn't do it. *You* did.

"I fell in with the wrong crowd."

This sentence would have us believe you just slipped and fell in. You didn't really want to. It wasn't really your choice. It was an accident that you joined the nude motorcycle gang. You just fell in.

"It spilled over into other areas of my life."

"It spilled over" is one more way to diminish the control and choice you have. It's a way to remove yourself from being in charge of the spillage and see yourself as unresponsible.

When I designed a regular exercise program for myself, I picked running. I created a running schedule and followed through on it. Over time, I proved to myself that I was a self-disciplined exerciser. Building on that success, I reasoned that if I could choose self-discipline in that area of my life, I could choose self-discipline in other areas of my life as well.

Using the feelings of power and control that I gained through running, I designed a regular writing schedule and stuck to it. I also changed my eating habits. I ate more healthy foods, in more healthy amounts, at more healthy times. As a result, I lost 15 pounds and finished the *Our Classroom* manuscript.

No way am I going to say my self-discipline "spilled over into other areas of my life." There was no "spilling" to it. I actively chose to exercise self-discipline in my writing and in my eating. It wasn't an accident, it wasn't luck, and it didn't "spill." I put self-discipline there on purpose, with intentionality. I love it and I'll take the credit, thank you.

"I just got hooked."

You can't be responsible for doing drugs. Not in this case. Not when a giant hook (one which you have no control over) drops out of the sky and forces you to do things against your will. It's certainly not of your own doing. You simply got hooked.

"My nerves are getting to me."

No, your nerves don't get to you. You get to your nerves. Blaming your nerves for an anxious reaction is like holding your hand accountable for striking an angry blow. "My hand did it," makes as much sense as, "My nerves did it to me."

I heard Arnold Palmer, the famous golfer, recently respond to this issue. Past his prime, and having not won a tournament in several years, an announcer was surprised that Palmer was leading this particular tournament. With two more rounds still to play, the announcer asked, "Arnie, do you think your nerves will hold up?" Arnie never hesitated. He responded with the sureness of someone who wore self-responsibility comfortably. "Oh, I've got the same nerves I had 20 years ago," he said. "My nerves are the same as ever, but my nerve may be different, though."

Arnold Palmer knew that his nerves were not responsible for his degree of calmness. He knew nerve was something *he* controlled, something for which *he* was responsible.

"Bob won't let me go out alone."

or

"My boss won't let me take a week off."

"Won't let me" is another phrase that assigns responsibility for your actions to an external source and erodes your sense of personal power. Do you hear yourself using it on occasion? Take a few minutes now to think about your own individual "They won't let me's."

Perhaps yours are job related. "My boss won't let me have the big accounts," or "The demands of this job won't let me relax." Or maybe yours are more personal. "They won't let me join the group," or "She won't let me look at other women."

Think of three "won't let me's" that are or have been true for you. Write them in the spaces below.

_____ won't let me _____.

_____ won't let me _____.

_____ won't let me _____.

34

Now go back and change your statements by replacing the first word with "I." Now the statements read:

"I won't let me join the group."

"I won't let me go out alone."

"I won't let me take a week off."

"I won't let me relax."

"I won't let me look at other women."

By using the word "I," you shift the focus away from the other controllers (they) and back to yourself. That choice of language increases the likelihood that you will examine the part you play in the creation of each situation.

While it may be true that your boss makes the final decision as to whether or not you take a week off, using language that leaves him in total control weakens your power and directs the focus away from the role you play in that decision. You are then not as likely to examine what it is *you* do to help create and perpetuate that situation, and are less apt to spend time examining what you can do to change it.

By saying, "They won't let me," you absolve yourself of all responsibility and assume nothing can be done. By saying, "I won't let me," you accept responsibility and are more likely to take positive corrective action.

"The mood overtook me."

This phraseology is intended to have us believe it's the mood's fault, as if the mood was separate somehow from the person choosing it. "It overtook me" means it took me over and I had no control. Therefore, I'm not responsible.

"I was swept up in anger."

Speaking of my anger in a way that describes it as being in control of me rather than me being in control of it is not useful. Using the words "swept up" helps me convince myself that emotions can't be controlled. And it gives me an excuse for not controlling my anger. How can I possibly be in charge of something so big that it can sweep me up?

"I was swept up in anger," gives the impression that anger is something that just happens to me, something over which I have no control. Actually, the opposite is true.

Moods and emotions are a result of how we choose to think about or interpret the events of our lives. They are caused by our past programming and our choice of thoughts. If we think happy thoughts, we are more likely to create happy moods. If we think sad thoughts, we are more likely to create sad moods. Moods, like our emotions as explained in Chapter One, are clearly under our control.

Often the language we choose helps disguise the choice we have over our feelings and moods. The more often you say, "The mood overtook me," or "I was swept up in anger," the more you reinforce your belief that you are not in charge. The more you strengthen that belief that you are not in charge, the more you behave in ways that reflect that belief.

If you don't think you choose your moods or your feelings, explain this situation.

A man and a woman are arguing in their kitchen. Loud voices trade accusations, denials, and threats. Menacing glances and closed body postures accompany the verbal attacks.

In the midst of these angry feelings, the phone rings. The man who answers immediately changes his tone and attitude. The conversation at this end then becomes, "Hi, Marge. Bridge next Thursday? Why, we'd love to. Thank you so much for inviting us. We had such a nice time last month. Who's coming? Great! I can hardly wait. Nice of you to call. Thanks again. Bye."

Immediately upon conclusion of the phone conversation, angry stances are reassumed and the argument continues, hotter than ever. As the illustration clearly indicates, we do control our emotions, our moods, and our feelings. We do it whenever it's convenient or whenever we want to. It's just that it's easier not to admit to ourselves that we have a choice sometimes. That way we don't have to be responsible.

It works the same with love. I recently asked a friend why he had purchased a dozen daisies. "I get really romantic when love strikes me," he replied. For some reason he chose to use language that hid the part he played in choosing or not choosing love. His choice of words described love as "out there" someplace, as if it were something that lurked around waiting to strike. He disowned responsibility for choosing love and described romance as an idea that happens to him on occasion if and when love strikes.

Actually, love is not something that waits out there like Cupid with a bag full of arrows. Love is an emotion that can only be experienced if you activate it. Love is within you. You have to flip the switch and turn it on. You choose love and you generate it. It's you who is in charge of the love or lack of love you feel at any given moment.

THE "HAVE TO/GOT TO/MUST" FALLACY

Using "have to," "got to," and "must" is one more way you reduce personal power in your life. Do these sound familiar?

"I *have to* get to work now."

"I've *got to* remember his birthday."

"I've *got to* help her with her homework."

"I *must* call my mother this weekend."

"Have to's" are self-limiting phrases that suggest you have no choice in the situation. They are absolutes that leave no room to negotiate. That choice of language reinforces your belief that you have no options and leaves you feeling powerless and out of control.

"Have to's" are not accurate. Actually, on close examination it becomes clear you really don't "have to" go to work now. There are several other options available to you, including:

1. You can call in sick.
2. You can quit.
3. You can say you overslept.
4. You can take a personal leave day.
5. You can just show up late with no explanation and take your chances that no one will notice.

No, you don't "have to" go to work now. You can choose any of the other alternatives and accept the resulting consequences. That's a choice you make every day. In reality, you are choosing to go to work, either because you want to or because you don't want to experience the consequences. Either way, it's your choice.

It's not helpful to talk to yourself as if you "have to" go to work. If you see it as a "have to," you won't enjoy it. It will seem like drudgery and you'll merely put in your time. When you say "have to," you can feel like a captive, someone who is being forced to submit to some terrible fate. It's no wonder you resist and don't enjoy work when you choose to speak of it as a "got to."

Speak of going to work as if it were the choice it is. "I'm choosing to go now," or "I've decided to work this morning," leaves you feeling more in charge. You'll experience more control and more power with that choice of language.

You don't really *have to* help her with her homework. You're choosing to do it because you like her and because you're a helpful person.

You don't really *have to* remember his birthday. You want to because you like him and you want to acknowledge that special day in his life.

You don't really *have to* call you mother this weekend. You can call her Monday night or even wait for her to call you.

Have To's and Anxiety

"Have to's," "got to's," and "must's" increase a sense of time urgency and contribute to hurry sickness. If I have to, I had better hurry. And hurry produces anxiety.

Creating anxiety by speaking to yourself as if you must learn some new concept or succeed at some activity in a hurry is harmful. Believing you must catch on to something quickly increases your chances of making an error.

Slow down. Relax. You don't "have to" anything. Take your time and choose. There's peace in knowing you choose and power in the act of choosing. Dump "have to's," "got to's," and "must's" and put more power and peace in your life.

By eliminating "have to's" from your language you will reduce anxiety, increase your awareness of the choices you make, and maintain your personal power.

"I've got to tell you this story," then becomes, "I'd like to tell you this story."

"You've got to understand," is changed to, "I want you to understand."

"I must interrupt here," is altered and comes out, "I choose to interrupt here."

The choice is yours. You can choose to speak in "have to's" or you can choose language that leaves you more in control. Remember, it's your choice. You don't *have to* do anything.

DEPENDING ON DEPENDENCY

To begin this section, I would like you to complete a sentence stem. Please write five different reactions to the sentence starter, "I need . . ." What do you need? Record whatever is true for you.

I need _____

I need _____

I need _____

I need _____

I need _____

If your sentences are similar to those shared by participants who have attended my workshops, your list of needs might include some of the following.

I need love and affection.

I need to lose 10 pounds.

I need more time.

I need more appreciation.

I need a new car.

I need more money.

I need a vacation.

I need new clothes.

Take a moment now and read your list aloud to yourself. Emphasize the word *need.*

Now go back over your sentences and cross out the word "need." Replace it with the word "want." "I need to lose 10 pounds," now becomes, "I want to lose 10 pounds." Do that for each *need* you have listed.

Now read your new "I want" statements aloud. This time emphasize the word "want."

How did that seem to you? Did replacing *need* with *want* change your sentences at all? Did it change the meaning or how you felt about them? Write your reactions here.

_____

_____

_____

I wish I could read your reactions or have you share them with me in person. I would like to know how you personally felt about this exercise. Participants who do this exercise in seminars generally report a wide variety of reactions. Their responses include:

"It didn't change it at all."

"I feel selfish with *want* in there."

"*Want* feels better because it's more accurate."

"I guess I really don't *need* those things. They really are *wants*, aren't they?"

"I don't like to go around wanting things all the time. It doesn't feel good."

Participant reactions generally fall into three categories — those who think *want* is more accurate; those who think *need* best describes their situation; and those who report no difference in the sentences. Where do you fit? Was your reaction similar to one mentioned above?

My reaction to this choice of words is based on my beliefs about personal power and the importance of self-responsible language. I believe there are only three real needs in our lives. We need food, water and love. If we don't have food or water, eventually we die. The same holds true for love, at least in our earliest years. If infants aren't stroked, cuddled, or loved, they die. Food, water, and love are basic needs. All the others are wants.

You don't really *need* a vacation. Certainly you *want* one. Probably you deserve one. And you'll survive without it. You might not like it, and you can exist without a vacation this year.

In the same sense, all of our supposed needs are actually wants.

I don't *need* a new car. I *want* one.

I don't *need* attention. I *want* attention.

I don't *need* more money. I *want* some, though.

I don't *need* your help. I *want* it.

Need and Dependency

"I need" and "I want" are ways to describe the desires in our lives. They are different words that send different messages. As you read the remainder of this section, think about unspoken, silent messages you send when you use need or want.

"I need" is a whiney phrase. It signals dependency. The more you need something, the more dependent you become. When you are dependent on anything in the outside world, you give your personal power away.

If you need her to be happy, you transfer the responsibility for your happiness to her. If you need a new job to be self-fulfilled, you transfer the responsibility for your self-fulfillment to the job. If you need recognition from others, you transfer the responsibility for recognition to others.

"I need" has expectations attached to it. When you announce "I need" something, it's as if you expect someone else to fulfill that need for you. Since you expect your need to be met, you assume a more passive stance and aren't as likely to work toward satisfying your desire.

"I want" is a more self-sufficient expression. It signals independence. It is simply a statement of desire with no expectation attached to it. Because you don't expect someone else to satisfy your desire, you assume a more active stance and are more likely to work toward fulfilling it.

In the middle of explaining this concept to my graduate class one night, a student challenged me with, "You probably don't even need your wife, do you?" The implication was if I don't need her, I don't love her. Of course I don't need my wife. And I do love her. I want her and I respect her tremendously, and I don't need her.

Don't misinterpret here. I want my wife very much. I want her as a friend, lover, business partner, and as a companion. And I would experience a deep sense of loss if she were not in my life. However, I can and would survive without her. I wouldn't like that, and I could do it.

And it works both ways. I don't want my wife needing me either. I don't want a woman who is dependent, clinging and living in my shadow. I want a woman who is independent and self-assured, someone who is responsible for herself and who likes it that way.

41

I want my wife wanting me in a variety of ways. I want her to want me to listen to her. I want her to want me to assist in workshop planning. I want her to want my opinion, my friendship and my attention. I want her to want me in bed. I want her to want all those things, and I don't want her to need them.

Think it over. Do you want someone who wants you or someone who needs you? Or perhaps you're like the singer in the country song I heard recently who wailed, "I need you to need me."

Approval

Look at the difference between wanting and needing approval. If I need approval, I'm more anxious to please. I'm careful not to say things that people might disagree with. I try to line myself up with the majority and appease the minority. I attempt to placate and get agreement.

If I need approval, I'm more likely to compromise my beliefs and sacrifice my self-interest. I agree when I don't really agree. I apologize frequently, and since I am more likely to cater to the wishes of others, I open myself up to be taken advantage of or used. I increase the chance that I can be manipulated.

When I want approval, I act differently. I don't measure my self-worth by others' reactions to me. I simply notice reactions and take them in. I process the data and am not immobilized by it. I'm not thrown off course for two weeks if I don't get approval.

Manipulation

Need is also an effort to manipulate. Ever hear these lines? "I need you?" or "I need it tonight."

These are attempts to "make you" feel guilty. They are efforts to "make you" feel responsible for satisfying someone else's desires.

If I were single and huddled with a friend in intimate surroundings and she said to me, "I need you," I'd get up and run. I don't want to be needed. I don't want to be responsible for fulfilling someone's desires, sexual or otherwise. I'm not interested in becoming involved in a dependent, manipulative relationship. Now, on the other hand, if I were in the same set of circumstances and the person said, "I want you," I'd be tempted to reply, "Oh, tell me more. Let's sit down and talk this over."

What do you like to hear? How do you want your lover talking to you — "I need you" or "I want you?" What sounds the juiciest to you?

Self-full-ness

Occasionally, workshop participants tell me that *want* sounds selfish to them. "Who wants to go around saying, 'I want this,' 'I want that' all the time?" they question.

I make a distinction between selfishness and self-full-ness. Selfishness to me is when I do my thing and I don't care what happens to you or anyone else. I don't advocate that approach and stating "I want" does not imply agreement with it.

I do believe in self-full-ness. I believe we nurture best from overflow. If I'm feeling full, I have more to give to my children, my spouse, my work, my colleagues, and to the cosmos. If I'm not feeling full, I don't have as much to give.

When I'm feeling empty or low, I'm less likely to be concerned with giving to others. Since I'm not full of self-esteem, energy, or positiveness, I use what I do have for myself. There's not enough left to share with the important people in my life.

When I take care of myself by satisfying some of my wants, I have more to give to others. If I buy a new sweater and I'm feeling good in it, I have more positiveness to share. If I get my hair cut and I'm feeling attractive, I have higher self-esteem and am more likely to treat others well. If I take an hour for myself to soak in the bathtub and end up refreshed and relaxed, I have more energy to put out to the universe. Since how I treat others is related closely to how I feel about myself, it may well be a disservice to those I love not to take care of myself and satisfy some of my own wants.

It's also important to fit my wants into the context of interdependence. Certainly it's important and useful for me to spend some time and dollars on myself. I deserve it and it helps me be self-full. On the other hand, I want to balance that

43

approach with the idea that every dollar or hour I spend on me is one less dollar or hour I have to share with my children and my wife. Each decision I make about satisfying my wants I temper with the realization that we as a family are connected.

Giving Information

"I want's" are not the whiney tones of a spoiled child. They are direct communication from a mature adult who believes in giving information. When I share my wants, I share them to let you know what I'm thinking and feeling. I don't share "I want's" with the attitude that I "have to" have it or even that I expect to get it. I share it as a way of giving you information about me so we can begin a useful dialogue between us. My approach is, this is what I want. Tell me what you want or react to what I want. Then let's talk it over and see if we can reach agreement.

Saying "I want" is another way of saying "I'd like it if" or "I would prefer it if." I find that when I tell people what I would like or what I prefer, I usually get it.

"Randy, I want you to chew gum outdoors."

"Jenny, I want you to turn down the volume of your radio."

"Bill, I want you to listen more attentively when I talk to you."

"Matt, I want you to wash the dishes tonight."

When I am clear about what I want, people generally respond. They respond by helping me attain my want or by sharing a want of their own. In each case, the situation is healthy because we have created a nondemanding, clear style of communication with one another.

Examine the difference between stating a want ("I want you to sit down") and making a command ("Sit down"). When you state your want, you simply give information and leave the choice of response to the other person. You assume responsibility for your want and let the other person be responsible for her response. You have room to negotiate.

When you command, you assume a position of authority and take responsibility for the other person's response. You disempower that person and leave no room to negotiate.

If you command and make demands of me, I am more likely to resist, resent, and refuse. If you tell me what you want, I may or may not agree. However, we will have a better chance of working it out.

Occasionally, others hear an "I want" as a demand. This happens because they are used to hearing commands and don't interpret the "I want" as a sharing of information. I believe it's important to work with these people by continually sharing what you mean by "I want." Over time they come to understand your intention and hear "I want's" in the spirit in which they are sent, as information about you.

A participant who recently completed one of my "Talk Sense" workshops wrote me with the following information on this issue. She said, "Sharing wants particularly hit home with me. I've often said 'I want . . .' and people interpreted my comments as being selfish. I started letting other people's judgments minimize the 'I want' statements in my life. Then I realized that some of the people didn't understand my intent. When I explained to them that my 'I want' statements were simply a way of stating information about myself and that they could respond to this anyway they wished to, I found myself getting more of what I wanted. That sure beats sitting back and taking rejection personally."

Sharing Wants

Most of us don't live with or work with psychics. Yet we often act as if we do. We hang on to our wants, don't verbalize them, and then resent it if other people don't figure them out.

We expect people to read our minds, as if we had glass heads. We embrace thoughts like, "If you loved me, you'd know," and "If he really cared, he'd figure it out." Then when the other person doesn't figure it out, we resent it. We get angry at others for not automatically knowing what we failed to state aloud. So we say things like, "If you don't know, I'm not going to tell you."

One way to diminish your chances of getting what you want in life is to fail to verbalize those want's. If you're the only one who knows what you want, your odds of getting it aren't very high.

Some people don't get what they want in their lives because they're afraid to say "I want." They don't take the risk. For them, it's easier not to tell and resent than it is to tell and risk rejection.

One reason people fear rejection and prevent themselves from risking "I want's" is because they take rejection personally. They follow a rational statement with an illogical conclusion about themselves.

For instance, when I say to Dee, "I'd like you to scratch my back," and she replies "I don't want to," her rational statement is simply "I don't want to." It's important that I don't follow her rational statement with illogical self-talk such as, "She doesn't love me," or "I'm not a worthwhile person."

Her statement tells more about her than it does about me. It may mean she's tired. It may mean she's busy. Or it may mean she just doesn't feel like it. Whatever her statement, it's about her. It's not about me. I don't have to take it personally.

Do you have some unexpressed wants? Take a minute now and get in touch with them if you do. Respond by completing the following section.

1. At work I want _____
_____
_____

2. I would like to say I want _____
_____
_____ to my parents.

3. One thing I want someone else to do for me is _____
_____
_____

4. A material object I want is _____
_____
_____

5. One thing I want people to know about me is _____
_____
_____

6. At home I want to have less _____
_____

7. I want my next vacation to be _____

_____

_____

8. For my birthday, I want _____

_____

_____

9. One thing I've always wanted to do is _____

_____

_____

10. I want to say _____

_____

_____ to _____

Look over your list. Place a star by the three that seem the most important to you right now. Pick one to implement today.

Speaking Collectively

Another language technique for increasing self-responsibility is to speak for yourself. Consider the following:

"*People* resent those things."

"*We* don't like that."

"*You* feel scared when something like that happens."

"*Parents* care about their children."

Each sentence above contains a word that represents "I and others." The italicized words are examples of speaking collectively, surrounding yourself and your statement with support from imagined others. The others are used to bring more clout to the statement, as if your feeling or opinion is not enough.

"We don't like that," is an admission that your voice has to have support to give it meaning and importance. It's like saying, "I'm not enough, but if I surround myself with all these other people (we) maybe you'll think my opinion is important."

It's an example of not speaking for yourself and diminishes your personal power. It's an unself-responsible style of communicating.

A helpful alternative to "I and others" is to eliminate the others. Use the word "I" and speak for yourself.

"I don't like that," tells how you feel about the situation. It's a sharing of your feelings and is an effort to let others know where you stand. It's an example of speaking for yourself and has a ring of personal power to it. It's a self-responsible style of communicating.

"*I* resent that," is more self-responsible than, "*People* resent those things."

"*I* feel scared," maintains more personal power than "*You* feel scared when that happens."

"*I* care about my children," is more powerful than "*Parents* care about their children."

Not surrounding yourself with the imagined support of others leaves you more alone. Yet it is the process of standing alone that creates self-sufficiency. Self-sufficiency helps you feel more self-responsible. Those self-responsible feelings in turn help you experience more personal power. With increased feelings of personal power you become more comfortable standing alone.

Another form of speaking collectively is "Me-too-ism." "John thinks we ought to go and I agree," is one example. "Sharon goes along with me on this," is another. Adding others to your view is a way to weaken your self-power. It tells your listener that your confidence and convictions are not strong enough to stand alone. You communicate to others and more importantly, to yourself, that you must use John or Sharon as a crutch.

Speak for yourself. Use language that reflects a view of yourself as independent, strong, standing alone. One way to do that it through the use of "I" statements.

"I" Statements

Somewhere in my education I was taught to eliminate *I's* from my writing and my speaking. I came to believe that many *I's* were a measure of my selfishness or a sign of my inflated self-importance. I struggled valiantly for years in an effort to find and use appropriate replacements. I was not always successful.

Today I have come to a different view of the word "I." I now believe it is the most self-responsible word in our language. I advocate increasing its use in several situations.

I believe that self-responsibility can be increased by using the word *I* to replace *it* and *it's*. *It* and *it's* are typically used to report conditions.

"*It's* cold in here."

"*It is* hot in here."

"*It* bombed out."

"*It's* amazing."

"*It is* uncomfortable at their house."

"*It's* exciting to do that."

"*It is* scary to go on roller coasters."

"*It* worked!"

It's and *it* are inaccurate, impersonal, and unself-responsible. When you say, "It's hot in here," your assumption is that everyone in this room feels exactly the same way you do concerning the temperature. You deny that your reactions are personal and that your experience is unique to you. Once again, you lump yourself in with others.

"I am hot in here," is more accurate than, "It is hot in here." Not everyone is hot. Chances are some people are cold, others just right. Saying, "It's hot in here," is putting responsibility for how you experience the temperature on the temperature. With those words you don't take the full responsibility for your feelings.

"I'm uncomfortable at their house," allows you to assume more responsibility for your feelings than, "It's uncomfortable at their house."

"I'm excited," is an expression that reveals greater ownership of your experience than, "It's exciting." "I'm scared to go on roller coasters," is more honest and personal than, "It is scary to go on roller coasters." "I worked it," gives you more credit than, "It worked."

CONCLUSION

The ideas and suggestions contained in this chapter, if used regularly, will help you to speak in more self-responsible ways. None of the suggested words or phrases used exclusively will immediately change your way of thinking or reacting. Together they will have a cumulative effect. Try them on. See which ones fit for you.

Spend some time listening to your language this week. Keep track of how often you speak with the language of self-responsibility. Write down the words and phrases you use that are not self-responsible. Work at changing those phrases and using language that leaves you in charge.

One advantage of purposefully choosing your own words is that every time you do that you reinforce your ability to be self-directed. When you use speech that you have intentionally designed, you remind yourself that you are a person who has the capacity to manage his or her own mind. You see yourself as the one who is in charge of programming your own life.

Chapter Four

THE LANGUAGE OF POSSIBILITY

"I can't swim very well."
"I can't seem to lose 15 pounds."
"I can't stop loving him."
"I can't find enough time."
"I can't take my eyes off of her."
"I can't get organized."
"I can't stand it."

"I can't" is the predominate self-limiting phrase used in our culture. It is a clear example of how people limit themselves through choice of language.

Of course you can get organized. You're just choosing not to right now. Certainly you can lose 15 pounds. All you have to do is design and implement a program of regular exercise and diet. Clearly, you can stand it. In fact, you already have for years.

Your not losing 15 pounds, your not being organized, and your not standing it have nothing to do with can't. They have to do with choices and priorities, the decisions you make about how to live your life.

Most "I can't's" are a lie. They are simply not true. They are a way you have of talking to yourself so that you don't have to take responsibility for the decisions you make. It's a language technique for keeping issues away from yourself, out there at a safe distance. It's a way of disowning and getting yourself off the hook. After all, if you *can't*, then how could you possibly be responsible?

When you say, "I *can't* come over right now," you choose language that implies no choice on your part. Your words paint a picture of yourself as a victim of circumstances, as someone who is out of control. Actually, you could come over right now if you wanted to badly enough. Perhaps you are choosing not to come over because you're in the middle of lunch and have three activities planned for the afternoon. You could skip lunch. You could cancel your other plans. It's not that you can't. You really are making a deliberate choice not to come over.

When you say, "I *can't* stop loving her," you pick words that deny you are in control of your loving and absolve yourself of all responsibility for your attitude and actions. Certainly you can stop loving her. Loving is a choice you make. You're not stuck loving her the rest of your life. You can move your energy and your attention to someone else if you want to. What you really mean when you say, "I can't stop loving her," is "I don't want to stop loving her because it's fun to feel bad," or "I don't want to spend the time and energy necessary to change my current programming."

An "I Can't" Activity

Think about times when you've recently said, "I can't," or when you thought the words silently to yourself. What have been your "I can't's"?

Please use the following exercise to increase your awareness of the power of "can't." Begin by completing the four sentence starters with statements that are, or have been, true for you.

Do this exercise with beginner's eyes. Do it as if you had not read the first part of this chapter. Record your own individual "I can't's" now.

I can't _____.

I can't _____.

I can't _____.

I can't _____.

If you've done this task with a degree of self-honesty, your "I can't" statements are probably similar to those I've heard from workshop participants around the country. They list statements like:

I can't quit smoking.
I can't stand my neighbor.
I can't pass up chocolate.
I can't think of any.
I can't play golf well.
I can't get my son to come home on time.
I can't find enough money to buy new clothes.

Whatever your statements, take the time now to read them aloud. Pay attention to how they sound. Emphasize the word "can't." Do it now.

To begin the second part of this exercise, go back to your statements and cross out the word "can't" in each one. Replace it with "don't." Now your statements read,

"I don't quit smoking."
"I don't stand my neighbor."
"I don't pass up chocolate."

When you have "don't" substituted for "can't," again read your statements aloud paying attention to how they sound. Emphasize "don't." Did you notice any change? Did the word "don't" alter your statements at all? How did you feel about them? Write your reactions here.

_____

_____

_____

_____

_____

Some people report they don't like "don't" in their statements. "Don't" helps them to become aware of the part they play in choosing cigarettes or chocolate. They prefer to believe they can't. For them, it's more comfortable to say "can't" than to admit they have a choice and are choosing not to.

Other people report a preference for "don't." They suggest "don't" leaves them feeling more powerful and in control. "Don't" feels more like a choice to them and they prefer the feelings that come from knowing they're in control.

What is your reaction to "don't?" Did it fit for you or feel uncomfortable?

For the next phase of this exercise, cross off all the "don't's" in your sentences and replace them with the word "won't." Your statements now will read:

"I won't quit smoking."

"I won't stand my neighbor."

"I won't pass up chocolate."

Once again read your new statements aloud. Emphasize the word "won't." Continue to pay attention to whether or not your statements change and how you feel about them. Record your reactions here.

_____

_____

_____

_____

_____

How did you react to "won't" in your statements? Did it fit some and not others?

Often workshop participants react strongly to "won't." Some don't like it. "It's too final," they say. They report "won't" sounds childish and whiney. Others think it has a stubborn ring to it.

Other participants prefer "won't." "It's a relief," they say. It feels to them as if they've already made a decision. They like the finality associated with "won't," the knowing that they have made a decision and are acting on it.

Those of you who have figured out how to play this game probably have already crossed out "won't" and are waiting for the next word to put in its place. If you haven't, please do that now. Then replace "won't" with the phrase "choose not to." Your sentences will now read:

"I choose not to quit smoking."

"I choose not to stand my neighbor."

"I choose not to pass up chocolate."

One final time please read your statements aloud. Emphasize "I choose not to." Again pay attention to how your statements sound to you and how you feel as you read them. Record your reactions here.

_____

_____

_____

_____

_____

Some participants enjoy the phrase "choose not to" and report that it helps them see the choices they are making in their lives. By changing their words from "can't" to "don't" to "won't" and then to "choose not to," they become more aware of the power inherent in language. These people often report they like the feeling of being in control that the new way of speaking offers.

Others at this point become defensive. They resist the notion that they are choosing and defend the language that limits. They either don't believe they are responsible for their "I can't's" or don't like the feeling of being responsible. For them it's easier to say they can't than to examine how they might be creating their own limits. "How can I choose to play golf well when I'm not coordinated?" they will question. Or, "I really can't afford a new car; how can you say that's a choice?" they will ask.

Golf is a physical and mental activity comprised of skills. Those skills can be practiced and learned. If you devoted hours of practice, piles of money, and chunks of perseverance to the task, you could learn to be an accomplished golfer. You're just choosing not to do that at this point in your life. You have different priorities and are making other choices. It's not that you can't play golf well. You just haven't done it yet. You are, by how you choose to live your life, choosing not to play golf well at this time.

Of course you can afford a new car. That might require you to change a few priorities in your life, though. You could sell your house and rent, or decide not to help your children complete college. You can get a part-time job in addition to your other work or use the equity in your house as security for a loan. You can get a new car if you really want one. Aren't you really choosing not to?

Real "I Can't's"

There are some "I can't's" that are real. For instance, I can't bear children without history-making surgery. I can't grow three feet taller and join the National Basketball Association. I can't swim across the Atlantic Ocean in two hours. These "I can't's" are real for me and are outside of my present reality.

Perhaps some of the "I can't's" on your list are real. Go back and look over your original list of "I can't's." Determine whether or not yours are real "can't's" or if they are decisions you make. Check them over carefully. We have been bombarded in our culture with a steady stream of "can't's" until many of us have come to believe falsely in our own limits. Are you sure it's a "can't" or could you do it if you wanted to badly enough?

A Language Lesson

The fallacy of "I can't" speaking and thinking was first explained to me by my friend, Tim Timmermann. Tim gave me my initial language lesson the day I met him. I picked Tim up at an airport, and began the process of getting acquainted during the fifty-mile ride to the site of his upcoming workshop. I mentioned that I enjoyed my ability to write, which up to that point consisted of two and three page vignettes about issues of concern to me. When Tim asked me if I had ever written a book, my reply was, "I can't write a book. It takes too long." He then responded with, "I'd like to ask you to change your mind about that," and I knew it was going to be no ordinary ride from the airport to the workshop site.

Tim explained that I really could write a book if I wanted to, and I agreed. He also shared how the language I used (I can't) got in my way and was part of the reason why I hadn't written a book. I agreed again. I learned a lot about the importance of language that day and have since learned enough to have completed one book for educators, *Our Classroom: We Can Learn Together,* as well as this book on language.

I began examining my language more carefully after my conversation with Tim. I heard myself using can't's in areas of my life other than writing. I noticed I used can't's at home and at work. I heard them when I spoke them aloud or thought them to myself. I was surprised at both the frequency and the intensity of my use of that word.

I began to purposefully alter my language. Whenever I heard myself doing "I can't" talk, I substituted other words. By replacing can't with "don't," "won't," and "choose not to," I began to discover what I was really telling myself. Sometimes I meant *I don't* (I don't run a 26.2 mile marathon yet). At other times, I meant *I won't* (I won't do mountain climbing). And sometimes I meant *I choose not to* (I choose not to stand ethnic jokes). Seldom did I mean "I can't."

I learned important lessons as I worked on my own "can't's." I learned that I was far less limited than I ever imagined and that it was *me* more than anyone or anything else that defined those limits. I learned that one of the major ways I created those limits was through my use of language. And I learned I could lift those limits and add possibility to my life by changing my programming.

Can't and The Subconscious Mind

Constant use of "I can't" language affects your subconscious mind. That repetitious programming becomes firmly entrenched in your subconscious, turns into beliefs, and later manifests itself in ways in which you aren't even aware.

When you use the word "can't," you program your subconscious mind to hold pictures and beliefs of yourself as a person who can't. Every repetition strengthens your belief.

Once you believe you can't, your actions reflect that belief. When your actions flow out of your "I can't" belief, you don't succeed very often. Because you don't often succeed, you reinforce your "I can't" belief and prove it to yourself. Your proof serves to further strengthen your "I can't" programming.

Don't wear unhelpful grooves into your subconscious mind. Choose programming that creates positive beliefs.

Change your language and program your subconscious mind with words that are helpful. Use "don't," "won't," and "choose not to." They are enabling words, words that affirm your self-responsibility and help you to see the control you have over your stance towards life.

"I can" and "I am becoming" are additional words that can help you program your bio-computer in a useful way. Start speaking of yourself as a person who can and you'll believe you are a person who can.

You can step out of your limiting beliefs. You can add more choice and possibility to your life. You can be an "I Can" person. It all starts with your words, the language you choose to use. You can do it.

Advertising

Part of our programming comes from people eager to control our spending habits. Advertisers want us to believe we "can't" get along without their products and that we "can't" look good, smell good, or do good without their help.

T.V., radio, newspapers and magazines continually remind us of items we "can't" do without. I recently came across a full-page magazine advertisement describing, "Something for everyone, Christmas gifts you can't resist." Among the objects I was being programmed to not resist were a Stir Crazy® popcorn/caramel corn maker, a Tonka® dump truck and Singer Tiny Tailor mending machine. I resisted.

Another magazine ad designed to appeal to me as a runner was created by the Hersey Custom Running Shoe Company. "Other running shoes don't make their shoes this way because they can't," stated the ad. It also suggested the following: "I think I make the best running shoe in the whole world. Because I do things that big companies can't afford to do, can't take the time to do, or haven't figured out how to do."

Recently, as I traveled on a local interstate highway, a large semi-truck passed me carrying a piece of programming. "Jay's, can't stop eating 'em," read the message. It apparently isn't enough for some companies to use the airwaves and print media to carry their messages. They're using trucks to deliver both products and programming simultaneously.

The Money Connection

Consider the following situation. Two customers are eagerly looking over winter coats that have just arrived at a clothing store. The prospective buyers are similar in many ways. Their financial status and ability to pay are identical. They have the same amount of cash on hand. Even their desire for a particular coat is equal. Only their words are different.

Person A tries on the coat, loves it, looks at the price tag and remarks, "I can't afford it." Person B tries on the coat, loves it, looks at the price tag and remarks, "I choose not to buy it."

Same situation. Same desire. Same decision. Different words. So what's the big deal, you may wonder.

The big deal concerns the words the customers used, the pictures they created for themselves and the beliefs those words reinforce.

Person A who says, "I can't afford it," is choosing a style of language that creates a picture of himself as a person without enough money. He is setting himself up as limited and living in lack. His words concentrate on not enough-ness. The message he sends himself is that he is not able to afford the purchase. He has little choice.

Person B, who made the same decision as person A, creates a different picture for himself by saying, "I choose not to buy it." His style of language produces an image of himself as a person who is acting prudently; someone who has executed self-will, and made a clear decision based on desire for the coat tempered with desire for other priorities. Also implied in person B's reaction is an attitude of abundance coupled with choice ("I can afford it and I choose not to").

Person A leaves the store with his head down, feeling poor, powerless and without choice. Person B leaves the store with his head high, congratulating himself on a wise decision, feeling abundant and powerful.

The point of this vignette is simple enough. Since the words you use lead to your feelings and actions, why not use words that leave you feeling powerful, abundant and full of possibility. Why not choose words that leave you in a place you like?

Other I Can't Variations

"I can't" is not the only phrase that chokes off possibility in your life. There are other synonyms that limit choice, confine thoughts and restrict your view of yourself. Some of them follow.

"I couldn't help it."

"I'd like to be able to do that."

"It's impossible."

"It's no use."

The above statements are *false.* They are false because you can help it if your desire is strong enough. You really are able to do "that" or anything else you set your mind to. It is possible if you devote the time, energy, and necessary resources. And there is "some use" if you believe there is.

The above statements are also *true.* If you really believe it's of no use, then it's of no use for you. If you believe deeply that it's impossible, sure enough, it's impossible for you. If you believe you're unable or couldn't help it, then you are unable and can't help it.

"Can't," "impossible," "not able" and "no use" are words that limit what you allow yourself to perceive and believe. You use them to do self-inflicted bondage. They help create the illusion that you are limited. Actually, there are no limits except those you set for yourself and those you acknowledge through your choice of language. Likewise, there *is* no such thing as limited people. There are only people who believe in limits. And beliefs about limits begin with limiting words.

Your words become your boundaries. They confine you by limiting your vision and your awareness of the possibilities that exist in your life. No one is capable of reaching for and achieving possibilities that they have already filtered out through restricting beliefs.

Your mind is where you create or inhibit your possibilities. And your mind is made up of words. It's time to take charge of the controls of your mind. It's time to intentionally program your own bio-computer with words that work for you, words that help you to sense choice, power and energy. It's time to limit the language of limitation and move increasingly into the language of possibility.

Other Self-Limiters

Matt, age seven, approached the refrigerator to help himself to some milk. "I probably won't find it," he said, referring to the milk. He stared at the shelves for 90 seconds and guess what? You're right, he didn't find any milk.

Sitting at the kitchen table with the rest of my family I rolled my eyes and sighed silently to myself. Seven years old and already my youngest son is setting himself up to fail with his language, using his own tongue to sabotage his efforts and create a mind set that proves to himself that he can't.

Why, I wondered, would he want to think he probably wouldn't find the milk? It's so much more useful and effective to think that he probably would find the milk. I didn't find a satisfactory answer to my question. I did find a solution, however.

I asked Matt to change his words. After a round of "Oh, Dad," he repeated the words I suggested. "I probably will find the milk," he said as he once again faced an open refrigerator. In less than 30 seconds he found the milk.

I was pleased that my lesson in language was effective and that the rest of my family overheard it. I was feeling productive, enlightened, and smug. Two minutes later I uttered a sentence that helped me realize Matt and I were in the same place, both learning and working at changing unhelpful verbal programming.

"It's going to be hard to run today," I said as I thought aloud about where to place exercise in the scheme of things I wanted to accomplish this day. Certainly, I had several other activities I wanted to complete. Yes, Randy and Jenny wanted me to drive them to soccer games. For sure, my legs were feeling heavy and tired. Still, why would I want to say, "It's going to be hard to run today?"

I don't want to use language that confines. I don't want to speak with words that argue for a narrowing of my possibilities. I don't want to believe that running at any time will be hard.

I immediately changed my words. "I'll find a time to run today," I said. As soon as I uttered the words, my rational mind began to review the day I had tentatively organized for myself, searching for a possible time to run. Instantaneously, my new language was helping create behavior that would produce my desired result, a time to run.

"Hard" was the word that signaled my self-restriction. It was the clue that helped me to open my mind and lift the limitation by changing my words. I was pleased I had recognized the clue. And it was during my 45 minute run that day that I chose to congratulate myself for noticing and changing my language.

Your words, too, contain clues as to the limits you're setting for yourself. You can hear them if you purposefully pay attention to your language. Hard, difficult, complicated, doubt, and their synonyms can serve as signals that you are programming your mind with unnecessary boundaries.

"It's going to be *difficult* to get this report done on time."

"These directions are *complicated.*"

"*I doubt* if I'll make the team."

Why would you want to believe it's going to be difficult to get the report done on time? Of course, it's going to be difficult if you believe it will be difficult. Why not use words that reflect a belief that if she wants the report finished by 10 a.m., she gave it to the right person?

Yes, the directions will be complicated if you tell yourself they will. It takes no more energy to believe the directions are easy than it does to believe they are complicated. Why use language that increases the likelihood that you'll have trouble understanding the directions? Why not think, "I can figure this out," or "One more reading and I'll have it"?

It will be much harder to make the team if you continue to program your mind with doubt. (See Chapter Six on The Language of Confidence.) You don't know whether or not you'll make the team. Why use words that plant doubt in your mind? Don't damage your chances by using words to create a mind that expects to fail. Why not choose language that reflects a belief in yourself or at least a "wait and see" stance?

Sometimes people challenge me here with, "But you're not looking at reality. What if I really don't have a chance to make the team?" Or, "These directions *are* complicated. Aren't you just trying to convince yourself of something that's not true?"

My reply is, "Aren't *you* convincing yourself of something that's not true?" What is true, anyway? *True* is what I believe to be true. If I believe the directions are complicated, it doesn't matter whether they are or not. Since I believe they are complicated, I act like they are complicated, and they in effect become complicated, for me. If I believe they are easy to understand, I act like they are easy to understand, approach them with confidence, and they become less difficult for me.

Even if the directions are complicated, why would I want to believe that? I prefer having them complicated and believing they are not, to having them easy and believing they are complicated.

It Isn't Easy

I quit drinking alcohol this year. Once I made the decision, I had little trouble following through on it. Beer, ice cream drinks, hard liquor and Chablis were easy for me to resist. Around Christmas time a friend brought over a bottle of Crackling Rosé. The bubbly pink stuff, my previous favorite, sat in the refrigerator for over a week before Dee popped the cork.

"It's not easy to pass up Crackling Rosé," I said as Dee poured herself a glass. We each heard my words, smiled at one another and jumped for paper to write down another example for this text.

Now why would I want to think it's not easy to pass up Crackling Rosé? If I believe it's going to be hard then it will be hard for me. I sure don't want to be inflicting myself with situations that are difficult for me. "It sure is easy to pass up Crackling Rosé," I said and we again smiled simultaneously.

The Always/Never Bind

Always and never swing both ways. They can be used to shut out and allow no options or they can be used to open up and increase possibility in your life.

"I *never* play well against him."

"I *always* have trouble with the first paragraph."

"Icy roads *always* cause me problems."

Using always and never in ways similar to those above gets in your way and clogs up your natural flow. Now, not only do you not play well against him, you *never* play well against him. With a mind programmed with that belief, what chance do you have?

You can raise the ceiling on your capabilities by using always and never to your advantage. Consider this programming:

"I *always* give people more than their money's worth."

"I *never* let down near the end."

"My mind *always* produces at least one good idea a day."

Never and always used in circumstances such as these pave the way for your achievement. They help you move beyond opening up possibilities in your life to a level of expecting and creating them.

Pay attention to the way you use always and never. They are weapons that you can use for or against yourself. Are you using them as servants or as detractors? Do they expand possibility in your life, or do they limit? Do they increase your personal power or shut it off? The choice is yours.

Nothing Is Too Anything

Webster's Seventh New Collegiate Dictionary lists the following definitions for "too." 1) also, besides; 2) a: excessively, b: to such a degree as to be regrettable, c: very. In the Moorman's First Self-Responsible Language Dictionary (as yet unpublished) "too" is defined as 1) a: limiter, b: preventer; 2) used as a defense and a rationalization for not taking responsibility for what I am or how I act.

"I can't do that. I'm *too* old."

"I'm *too* young. I don't have enough experience."

"I'm *too* mad to do it right now."

"That's *too* good to be true."

Too is a widely used word in our society. Variations abound.

> I'm too lazy.
> I'm too sad.
> It's too cold.
> I'm too tired.
> I'm too hot.
> I'm too excited.
> I'm too easy.
> It's too far.
> I'm too nice.
> I'm too fat.

That's too much.

I'm too slow.

I'm too frightened.

It's too expensive.

I'm too frustrated.

I'm too sick.

It takes too long.

Too is a primary preventer. People use it to prevent taking action and following through (it's too wet to mow the grass). They use it to prevent a view of themselves as able (I'm too old). They use it too prevent taking full responsibility for the way they act (I was too mad to say nice things to her). Some people use it to prevent risk or change (she's too good looking to ask for a date). And others used it to prevent failure (that's too hard).

Too is also an excuse. It is used as a defense to justify actions or inaction (it was too hot in that gym for me to perform well). It is used to rationalize a result (I was too nervous at the start of the game). And it is used to cop out (he was too upset with me so I didn't tell him).

Too is used in a variety of situations and most are related to limits. Most are also not true. The temperature may be 100°. Still it's not *too* hot to mow the grass. You could mow the grass in 130° temperature if you wanted to.

You're not *too* old to start jogging. Of course it's intelligent to consult a doctor and start slowly if you're past a certain age. Some people begin jogging at the age of 80. So you are not *too* old.

You're really not *too* tired to clean the garage. If someone called to invite you to a golf game, you'd be packed and out the door in five minutes. And your gait would reflect energy and enthusiasm. Cleaning the garage has nothing to do with being *too* tired.

Too is a word you can use to convince yourself of your limitations. The word, used repeatedly, helps structure your beliefs. Once the beliefs of I'm too old or I'm too scared are embedded in your bio-computer, they help determine your actions. And when you *act* old and scared you *become* old and scared.

Certainly you're frustrated. Still, you don't have to be *too* frustrated unless you decide to be.

Of course you're cold. Yet, you're not *too* cold unless you decide to create it that way for yourself.

Maybe you haven't chosen initiative in the past. Still what good does it do to talk to yourself as if you're *too* lazy?

And why would you want to believe it's *too* good to be true? Aren't you worth it? Nothing is *too* good to be true. In fact, nothing is *too* anything.

The language of possibility does not include "too." It's too limiting. (Sorry, I decided not to resist that.) To remove "too" from your language, it's important to notice those times you use it. When you become aware that you've used "too," an effective antidote is to repeat the sentence without it. Then add a phrase that describes your choice.

"I'm too tired to clean the garage," can become, "I'm tired and I choose (or choose not) to clean the garage."

"She's too attractive for me to ask for a date," could be "She's attractive and I choose (or choose not) to ask her for a date."

"It takes too long to drive to Florida," can be changed to, "It takes two days to drive to Florida and I choose (or choose not) to do it."

By dropping "too" from your language, you will expand your awareness of the possibilities that exist. Sometimes you may choose one of those possibilities. Other times you may not. Either way, you won't be hiding the decisions you make from yourself by placing the responsibility for those choices on "too" something. You'll be freeing yourself up to choose, increasing your personal power and using the language of possibility.

Dead Enders

There is one style of arranging language that shuts off possibility so quickly and permanently in your life that it deserves a special name. Choosing words in this category leaves you with no way out. I call them Dead Enders. Some follow.

"That's just the way I am."

"It's just a natural state of mind."

"I'm just a Pisces."

"I'm a morning person. What do you expect from me?"

"That's life."

"That's destiny."

"I'm just like my dad."

Each of these dead enders is a variation of "There isn't anything I can do." Each locks you into a set position from which there is no escape. Each is programming that diminishes your sense of personal power.

Dead enders limit your response-ability. Once you've said, "That's just the way I am," to yourself, you have decreased the possibility of making other responses. With those words, you convince yourself that there are logical reasons why you continue to make the same limited response. And since your rational mind continues to send you messages that support your programming, you stay trapped by a belief that is inaccurate.

I have a friend who argues frequently with his wife, his boss and his neighbors. I asked him why he argued so often and he told me, "I have a quick temper. It's just the way I am." His belief that his temper has a short fuse is well developed. He's been programming his mind with that illusion for many years. Naturally, his behavior is consistent with his false belief.

Because my friend believes he has a quick temper and because he believes that's just the way he is, he has limited response-ability. He continues to make the same response to similar situations over and over again. He gets angry and ends up fighting or arguing. My friend's choice of language helps perpetuate a picture of himself as someone who has no choice. And because his beliefs are firmly entrenched, he lacks the ability to make other, more effective responses.

In computer talk, the notion of response-ability is referred to as requisite variety. It means that if one side of a computer game is programmed with two responses and the other side given six responses, the side with six responses it going to dominate. The computer program with the ability to make the most responses will eventually win. It may take awhile, but the side with most available options will prevail in the end. It has more power and is more often a winner because it has a greater ability to respond.

Requisite variety works the same way with human beings. My friend, the arguer, is like the computer program with lim-

67

ited requisite variety. He has a narrow selection of responses from which to choose. Because he consistently chooses language that reinforces his belief that his temper is short, he eliminates many responses connected with holding his temper in check. No wonder he frequently ends up as a frustrated, angry loser.

If, through your choice of language, you continue to reinforce a belief that you are a morning person, you set yourself up to have less choice in the evening. If you continually argue that you are just like your dad, you lock yourself into a limited set of behaviors that imitate his responses to life. If you insist on using programming that strengthens your belief that jealousy, fear or frustration are just a natural state of mind, you prevent yourself from choosing more pleasant emotions in certain situations.

Dead enders limit your ability to respond. They cut off entire ranges of behavior by placing them outside of your belief system. They limit the perspective and choice necessary for you to experience the power inherent in a multiple option existence.

Variations

"I'm not mechanical."
"I'm not creative."
"I'm emotional."
"I'm a homebody."
"I'm not musical."
"I'm not religious."
"I'm sensitive."
"I'm not athletic."
"I'm not mathematical."

Be careful what you tell yourself. Each of the statements above is a variation of "That's just the way I am." Each programs your mind. Each limits your response-ability. Each reinforces the illusion that you are just that way.

Personal Dead Enders

What dead enders do you use? What limits do you create in your head by saying, "That's just the way I am"? List some of yours here.

_____

_____

_____

_____

_____

Change

Changing dead enders into the language of possibility begins with the act of noticing. If you don't notice when you use dead enders, there is nothing you can do to change them.

If you don't hear yourself say, "That's just the way life is," you are powerless to challenge the statement. If, "I'm easily upset," is not recognized as a dead ender, you will continue to limit yourself with it. Likewise, if, "My parents were that way," goes unnoticed, you cannot alter its effect on your bio-computer.

Listen for dead enders on T.V. and at the movies. Pay attention to the language choices of your friends, relatives and acquaintances. Start hearing dead enders from others and you will increase your ability to hear your own.

The purpose of being conscious of your language is to help you see and hear options in your life. Options result in more personal power. If you see many alternatives in a situation, you are more powerful than if you see few.

When you become conscious of your own dead enders, you will be in a position to do something about them. Examine them with ruthless scrutiny. Question your one-way statements. Is it really just the way you are or is it simply the way you were the last three times? Yes, you are Pisces, but do you have to act like a Pisces all the time? Do you really want to believe that "that's life"?

A useful statement to counter dead enders that I learned from my friend, Tim Timmermann, is, "It doesn't have to follow." I use the statement as a tool to negate dead enders as soon as I hear myself express one. It's a tool that helps me increase my own feeling of potency by helping me stay conscious of the choices I have.

When I hear myself say, "There's nothing I can do," or "That's just the way I am," I follow it with, "It doesn't have to follow." The new statement helps me remind myself that it doesn't have to be that way. There are other choices. I have other options available to me. Saying, "It doesn't have to follow," increases the likelihood I will examine all the possibilities of a situation. It helps me become more response-able.

Use "It doesn't have to follow" in your life. Check it out. See if it will work for you. If you're saying to yourself, "Those things never work for me," remember, *it doesn't have to follow.*

I Am

Sentences that begin with "I am" are powerful programming that can cement erroneous beliefs into your consciousness. Those words help you identify with the condition that follows them.

"I am ill."

"I am exhausted."

"I am nervous."

If you say, "I am ill," you identify with illness. You send programming to your bio-computer that focuses on illness. And since you become more like those conditions and characteristics you identify with, you invite more sickness into your life.

Concentrate on illness and you feel more ill. Concentrate on health and you feel more healthful.

If you're sick, stop talking about it. Stop giving it your attention, your energy and your words. Simply refuse to identify with it. Think about, talk about, and picture health instead.

Talk about where you do feel good. Verbalize what you can do. Let your words emphasize improvement. Concentrate on well-being. Identify with health and attract more of that condition into your life.

Some people use language to identify with old age.

"I'm over the hill."

"I'm not what I used to be."

"I may be giving away my age, but . . ."

"It must be my age."

The more you use words to acknowledge your aging, the more power you give it in your life. The more you talk about how old you're getting, the more you program yourself to feel and act old.

Stop talking about age and let your words reflect youth. Speak of the energy you feel, the youthful spirit that exists and the vitality you experience. Use language that helps you activate your body and mind with youthful energy.

Talk about youth. Think about it and picture it. Program your bio-computer with youthful messages and watch your body and spirit feel and act increasingly youthful.

"I am" is a clue. What follows that phrase is important programming. When you say, "I am tired," you program yourself to be more tired. If your words are, "I am energized," you use programming that helps you feel more energized.

Programming For Anxiety

An experience I had recently will help me illustrate how I used words to identify with a condition and how that condition was strengthened through the use of language. Dee and I were preparing to be guests on a talk show to promote our book for teachers, *Our Classroom: We Can Learn Together.* We had never appeared on a talk show and didn't know what to expect. Would the host be gentle or controversial? Would he agree with us or argue? What kind of calls would we receive? We had no idea.

As the date for our radio appearance approached, I noticed some faint rumblings in my stomach. I could tell I was creating anxiety. In an effort to alleviate my anxiety, I approached friends who had previously been on talk shows to inquire about their experience. In each case, I shared with them "I am" statements. I told them, "I am scared," "I am nervous," or "I am anxious." The effect of my words and conversations was to become even more nervous, anxious and frightened.

The day before our scheduled appearance, I realized what I was doing. I noticed my language and heard how I was identifying with fear. No wonder I was becoming increasingly anxious. I was reinforcing the condition by talking about it with anyone who would listen.

I decided to change my words. Instead of describing and labeling what was going on inside of me as anxiety or nervousness, I chose to call it excitement and anticipation. I replaced, "I am nervous," with "I am excited." I changed, "I am filled with anxiety," to "I am filled with anticipation."

I used those new words with several friends that day. Steadily, I felt changes occurring in my body. I became less tense, my stomach muscles started to relax, and I began to breathe more deeply.

I began to identify with excitement rather than fear, anticipation instead of anxiety. And I began to look forward to the show.

By simply changing my words, I changed my internal experience from fear to excitement. Through the use of language, I created a new perception which resulted in a new reality for myself. I ended up enjoying the talk show, myself and the entire process.

Listen to your words. Pay attention to what you're identifying with. Are you identifying with health, energy and abundance? Or do your words reflect illness, tiredness and lack?

THE LANGUAGE OF UNITY

Our language is full of words and phrases that divide, separate and compartmentalize. These word choices limit both vision and possibilities. I call that style of speaking the language of dichotomy. It works in opposition to the language of unity.

"But"

"But" is the smallest member of the language of dichotomy and is also one of the most powerful. It symbolizes a fascination with either/or thinking and is one more way we limit ourselves.

"But" appears harmless enough at first glance. It's generally used as a connector or to contrast two parts of a sentence. How could it possibly be limiting? Let's look closer.

"I like your report *but* it's longer than I wanted."

"I enjoy going out to dinner *but* it costs a lot."

"I want to go to Florida for spring training, *but* I don't have enough money."

"But" is designed to separate ideas. It divides and creates distance between two parts of a sentence. It leads us into perceiving situations as either/or. By using "but" we are more likely to act as though the two parts of the sentence are mutually exclusive.

"But" has a ring of finality about it. When I say, "I want to go to Florida for spring training," I sound powerful. Possibilities abound. When I add, "but, I don't have enough money," I dilute my personal power and view my desired trip as improbable.

We can step out of either/or thinking and increase our sense of personal power by changing one word in our language. Use "and" to replace "but."

"I'd like to go to spring training *and* I don't have enough money."

"I like your report *and* it's longer than I wanted."

Hear the difference? "And" is a word that combines ideas rather than separates them. It pushes ideas together rather than pulls them apart. "And" helps us see the whole picture rather than concentrating on the limiting components.

Read the following sentences aloud.

A. "I want to call her for a date but it's late."

B. "I want to call her for a date and it's late."

In each case, the wanting is strong and sounds powerful. In example A, "but" weakens the wanting by connecting it to a limiting factor. "But" implies restriction. There seems to be no choice. In example B, "and" combines the hindrance with the wanting and does not necessarily imply restriction. The wanting remains strong. Choice is more apparent.

If I say, "I want to publish this book, *but* I don't have a publisher," I'm more likely to feel defeated. I'm less likely to see options and less likely to take positive action.

If I say, "I want to publish this book *and* I don't have a publisher," I'm more likely to start looking around to see what I can do about it. I'm more likely to perceive possibilities and take positive action.

Us vs. Them

Black/white, man/woman, Democrat/Republican, Catholic/Protestant, American/Russian, white collar/blue collar are all examples of words that place people in categories. Divorced, single, young, midwesterner, communist, Jew, Hispanic, union and management are a few of the others that fill our language and our minds, and in turn influence our behavior.

When we use words like black and white, young and old, we divide people into groups of mutually exclusive sets. This use of the language of dichotomy results in rigid thoughts and rigid perceptions. Rigidity of any kind in our lives closes off options, reduces possibilities and limits.

Words that categorize people are divisive. They create separation in our minds. The mental separation leads to emotional separation. And emotional separation precedes physical separation. Once physical separation exists, the likelihood that rigid perceptions will be challenged or changed is greatly reduced.

Labels that categorize people cause separation by helping us see others as different. When our words announce differences, our minds perceive differences. When our minds dwell on differences, our actions reflect those differences.

When we see and think with minds that separate people into categories, we tend to generalize.

"Blacks are dirty."

"Old people are senile."

"Women are emotional."

"Teenages are lousy drivers."

"Russians are aggressive."

Generalizations become beliefs and influence our behavior. When we believe old people are senile, we act differently than we would if we believe old people are not senile. When we believe women are emotional, our actions flow in part from that belief.

By filling our heads with words that compartmentalize, we produce a mind that is less flexible and less likely to see options. Judgments are made more quickly as issues are lumped into right and wrong. Situations are perceived as good or bad. People are sorted into friends or enemies.

When we speak and think in dichotomous terms, we seldom see two sides of an issue, much less all the area that is in between. We severely limit ourselves with our thinking. We narrow both our perception and our range of possible responses.

When our beliefs center on right/wrong, good/bad, friends/ enemies, we become easily upset with others. Being right takes on a greater importance than finding solutions. Judging holds more value than accepting. Suspicion dominates trust. And conflict outweighs compromise.

Survival as a Species

The "us vs. them" or "me vs. you" mentality may have served us well at one time in our evolution as a species. If it ever did, those days are now over. Our survival on this planet now depends on our desire and ability to step out of mental habits that produce us/them behavior and cultivate an us/we/ our consciousness.

"Us vs. them" thinking has produced the bomb. It continues to produce behaviors that stockpile and devise new weapons at a rate that has moved beyond crisis proportions. It could well be responsible for the purposeful or accidental triggering of a holocaust.

The language of dichotomy is taking us down the road of mutual destruction. By using words that focus on our separateness as nations, we develop strong beliefs in our differences. Those beliefs result in suspicion, misunderstanding, competition and conflict. The ultimate action, the pressing of a button, could come at any moment.

No one can win a nuclear war. When it comes to ending life on this planet as we know it, being right doesn't work. We will sink or swim together. Yet we continue to use words and produce thinking that pits *us* against *them,* creating greater separateness in our minds and in our hearts.

The crisis of our time demands new words, new thinking and new ways of seeing. It is time for the language of unity, for words that reveal a common humanity, for thinking that speaks to our connectedness, and builds on our similarities.

Separation is a state of mind. So is unity. Both begin with words. It's your programming that creates your reality that others are different from you. And programming can create a reality that others are similar.

Actually, we are more alike than different. Our sameness outweighs any cultural, physical, or social differences that exist.

Concentrating on separateness by using the language of dichotomy produces an us/them mental frame that increases our belief in differences. Concentrating on commonalities by using the language of unity will produce an Us/We/Our mental frame that will increase our belief in connectedness.

Whether a person becomes a "them" or an "us" for you depends on how you use language to arrange your mind. Consider the experience of an elementary teacher I know who was having trouble working effectively with her principal. As I listened to her describe her relationship with him, it became clear to me why she was experiencing a strained relationship. Much of her language revealed her perception of him as the opponent. Her words categorized him as management, administration, boss, and ex-jock. Her language was helping produce separateness in her mind. She saw and acted out a me vs. you existence with this person.

I suggested she change her language and move it from a concentration on divisivenss to a focus on inclusion. Us, we, our, team, are harmonizing words that could help her perceive togetherness and mutual interest.

As this teacher began to use the new words, she began to develop an us, we, and our consciousness. She began to see her principal as a human being, rather than the boss. Once she changed her programming, it wasn't long until her behaviors fell in line with her new way of speaking and thinking. Gradually, her relationship with the principal improved.

Us, We, Our

The language of unity eliminates words that divide people into mini-factions by lifestyle, social status, role, skin color, or nationality. It speaks of subgroups as part of a larger whole and concentrates on inclusion rather than exclusion. It is made up of words that create mental pictures of togetherness, cooperation and connectedness.

Us, we, and our are words that will help you see and think in holistic terms. They help bring people together in cooperation, harmony, and understanding. Management *vs.* union can be changed to management *and* union with the words "our company." Boss *vs.* workers can be altered to boss *and* workers through the use of "our team." The United States and Russia can be seen as "our world."

By eliminating words from your language that categorize, you can free yourself from partisanship and rigid thinking. You can look at people more as individuals and less as representatives of some group. You can reduce stereotyped ways of seeing, thinking and acting, and be freer to react to people as unique human beings.

Some of Us

A useful phrase for creating a mental picture of unity is "Some of us."

Some of us litter.

Some of us like cats.

Some of us use unself-responsible language.

Some of us rob banks.

Some of us are black.

Some of us are white.

Some of us root for the Yankees.

When I see someone throw paper out the window of their car while traveling down the highway, I'm tempted to activate programming that separates me from that person. I'm likely to judge, categorize, or do name calling. When I catch myself using the language of dichotomy which separates me from the other person, I employ the phrase "Some of us."

"Some of us litter," I say to myself. That phrase reminds me of our common humanity and helps me to focus on connectedness. It is an example of programming that is inclusive and prevents me from creating a "me vs. them" program in my head.

When you say, "some of us," it's like drawing a circle around you and the other person, focusing attention on commonality.

"Some of *us* like cats."

(me . . . . . . cat lover)

The language of dichotomy separates. "He likes cats and I don't," is like drawing a line between you and the other person.

"He likes cats and I don't."

me   /   cat lover

In this case, your words create a mental barrier that creates divisiveness and separation. In essence, you use words to drive a wedge between you and another human being. Be assured that your behavior will eventually match your words.

Other Enemies

People and nations aren't the only targets for separation into the mutually exclusive categories of friends and enemies. A colleague of mine speaks of snow as if it were her enemy. Her words describe snow as dangerous, a nuisance, and as something to do battle with. It's not surprising considering her programming that each winter she experiences several problems with snow.

Why speak of snow as an enemy? Why not embrace the snow? Use programming that talks about snow as a friend. Create a "me *and* snow" consciousness rather than a "me *vs.* snow" consciousness. Use language to help you lean into winter and enjoy it.

What do you set up as the enemy in your life? Computers? A university? Mechanical items? Your garden? Teenagers? The garage? Your neighbor's dog? You can figure it out if you pay attention to your language. Watch for programming that creates enemies. Then ask yourself if you really want to attract that kind of reality for yourself.

Removing the language of dichotomy from your life will create an inner flexibility. That inner flexibility will lead to an outer flexibility and liberate you from stereotyped acting and reacting. The result is you will have more possibilities for responding to people and events in your life. In essence, you will have become more response-able. You will experience more choice, increased possibility, greater freedom and a stronger sense of personal power.

Summary

Your language can imprison or free, include or exclude, encourage or discourage. It can help you see multiple options or it can limit alternatives. It is a tool you can use for or against yourself, to add or subtract possibilities in your life.

Can't, difficult, hard, never, always, too, that's just the way I am, but and *the language of dichotomy* are examples of words and phrases that may be preventing you from experiencing a life full of choice, rich with possibilities. Listen to yourself. What do you hear yourself saying? Your words are convincing you of something. Do you like what they are telling you? If not, you can limit your limiters by choosing words that reveal your alternatives. You can learn to speak with the language of possibility. It's your choice.

Chapter Five

LANGUAGE OF ACCEPTANCE

"It was my best 10,000-meter run this year. Still, I was 20 seconds behind Bill."

"She's an awful boss. What a lousy manager."

"That was a terrible mistake. How could I ever be so dumb?"

The words above do not reflect the language of acceptance. They blame, criticize and compare. Their use signals feelings of inferiority, the need to be right, and limited perception. They are a sign that the speaker is caught in the Judgment Trap.

THE JUDGMENT TRAP

The Judgment Trap begins with our rush to evaluate. We compare, rate, score, judge, and assign value to movies, oranges, meat, music, furniture, cars, people, animals, and baseball teams.

We grade eggs and children. We assign numbers to horses and women. We rank order television programs, tennis players and lovers. We identify the world's best dressed men, determine the top 20 college basketball teams, and choose a Miss Universe.

We talk about good and bad, beautiful and ugly, skinny and fat. We notice gorgeous, awful, lousy, stupid, wonderful, fair, nice, smart, best, better, the greatest, the worst, least, lower, and O.K.

We evaluate our jobs, our co-workers, our families, our friends, and ourselves. Nothing it seems, escapes the critical, judgmental, evaluative mindset of our culture. We even evaluate the weather.

Our parents began our training in evaluation the day we were born. Within minutes of our birth, we were talked about as beautiful, cute, strong, excellent, healthy, ugly, homely, weak, poor, or unhealthy. We were told throughout our early years how good we were when we walked, talked, and went "potty" in appropriate places.

When we got to school, the evaluation parade lengthened and intensified. We were rated on our speech, grouped according to our reading level, and assigned grades for our performance in math, science, and spelling, We got stars, stickers, smiley faces, or red pencil marks on our papers. We were tested and ranked by percentiles, I.Q.'s, and mental maturation. Our parents conferenced with teachers to hear how we compared to others.

In high school, the judgments continued. College preparatory, business or vocational education were the new labels. Honor rolls, eligibility lists and class rankings told us where we stood. We tried out, got cut, or made the team. We were judged as being in or out of "the" group.

Yes, by the time most of us became young adults, we had been well trained in the process of evaluation. For many of us, judgment, comparison, and the rating game had become a way of life. Without our conscious awareness or consent, we had become caught in the judgment trap.

Judgment has become commonplace in our culture. From birth we have been trained to participate in the process. We have been taught to use it, expect it, and to view it as useful and necessary.

Because judgment has become such an integral part of our living, it could be easy to mistake its confinement. It could be easy to accept it as an innocent part of our lives without questioning its value or effect. And it could be easy to stay caught in its grasp.

Judgment is a trap. It limits vision and narrows perspective. It works against us by keeping us prisoners of our own judgmental language. Consider what happens when people judge something as common as the weather.

The Weather

Perhaps you've heard or used phrases like the ones that follow.

"What a lousy day."

"More good weather is on the way."

"We had awful weather on our vacation."

When you label the day as lousy, you have made a judgment about the weather. Your judgment is not only inaccurate, it helps perpetuate your illusion about the day and sets in motion forces that create for you a reality that matches your choice of language.

Actually, the day comes to you with no evaluation attached to it. Even though the weather forecaster talks as if the day is good or bad, beautiful or terrible, the day is simply the day. It just comes to you as it is, free of judgment and evaluation.

When it rains and you use words that label the weather as bad, lousy, crummy or terrible, you narrow that day in your mind. Narrowing occurs because your words program your bio-computer to be constantly on the alert to send you proof that your judgment is correct. Your mind follows through and sends you an incessant stream of thoughts and perceptions in line with your judgment.

Because you've judged the day as lousy, your mind helps you focus on limitation. You think of all the things you believe you can't do. You dwell on opportunities lost. You imagine inconvenience and interpret rain as getting in your way, slowing you down or preventing you from completing goals. You activate separating emotions of sadness, irritation, disappointment, anger or disgust.

When you don't judge the rain and speak of it as rain instead of evaluating it, you widen the day for yourself. Descriptive as opposed to judgmental language does not create a mind intent on proving the weather is bad. Nor does it create a mind busy developing or strengthening beliefs about rain being lousy weather. Therefore, your bio-computer is free to send you a wider selection of thoughts, ideas and perceptions concerning the day.

Now you are more likely to think about taking a walk in the rain, completing some task that could be done inside, or enjoying the sounds of rain on the roof. Your mind, not limited by an evaluation, is now more likely to generate new possibilities about the day which increase your range of choices. And you are more likely to activate emotions of joy, peace, happiness or contentment.

Judgment of People

Judgment also limits how we see people.
"He doesn't care about anything."
"She is unorganized."
"That kid is dishonest."
When you judge another person as uncaring and use language that reflects your view, you reinforce a belief that the person is uncaring. Once again, you begin a series of mental processes designed to prove yourself correct. Your judgment serves as an internal alarm, ready to go off any time uncaring is perceived. Because of your programming, you are more likely to notice uncaring acts. In addition, caring acts often go unnoticed, or if noticed at all, are not interpreted as caring.

Over time, through selective noticing and biased interpretation, you narrow this person in your mind. You perceive and experience him as uncaring. You don't notice as often his compassion, organization, love, fear, doubts, or many of the other characteristics, traits, or abilities that go into the makeup of his humanness. This person in time becomes the label for you rather than a fully functioning human being possessing a wide range of behaviors and attitudes.

Judgment keeps you from seeing clearly. If you judge someone as old, you're not as likely to see behaviors that reflect youth. If you judge someone as ugly, you're not as likely to notice their beauty. If you judge someone as gifted, you tend to become preoccupied with their giftedness and miss the characteristics they have in common with others.

Judgment Categorizes

Judgment places people into categories. Categories leave little room for exception. If you judge your boss as unorganized, then you tend to look at her as unorganized. You don't notice that her desk or her exercise schedule is highly organized. Because you use words that lump her in the category of unorganized, your mind creates an all inclusive picture of her as "that way."

Judgment Makes Permanent

Judgments also permanentize. They tend to be self-fulfilling and final. If you judge a child as dishonest, and use language that communicates that belief to him, you increase the chance he will be dishonest. If you create someone as clumsy in your mind, they tend to become clumsy in the reality you create for yourself. They then have to become extra-honest or extra-coordinated before you release them from your judgment trap.

Judgments Are Often Inaccurate

Judgments are not only a trap, they are usually inaccurate. We generally don't have enough information to make accurate judgments.

If I told you a man sitting on a bus failed to give his seat to a pregnant woman carrying packages, you may judge him as inconsiderate. If I explained further that he wore dark glasses and carried a white cane, you might make a different judgment. If you learned later that he was only impersonating a blind man, you'd have still another judgment.

When you judge another person, you judge him on the basis of insufficient evidence. You don't know what it's like to be inside another person's skin. There is no way you can see life through his eyes. You have not lived his experiences.

We are limited in what we can take in through our computer-like brains. We do not see, hear, and experience everything. We see only a portion of what goes on and glimpse only a part of what a person really is. And yet we often judge that person as if what we see is the total and final picture.

We have one meal and judge the chef as a good cook. We watch the rookie strike out three times in his first game and call him a bum. We have one positive experience with an airline and rate them as superior.

Judgments are always based on insufficient evidence, regardless of the length of time we've known a person or a situation. I've known my parents for over forty years, yet I don't really know what it's like to be them. What is it like to face retirement and live out the later years of life? I don't know. What was it like to be young and in love in the middle of World War II? I don't know. What was it like to watch one of your three children die of muscular dystrophy? Again, I don't know. I don't know all my parents' hopes, fears, concerns, and goals. I didn't live their life's experiences. They did. I know a lot about my parents, and I don't know everything.

Judgment Is About You

Another aspect of judging that could use closer examination is that judgment reveals more about the judge than it does about the person being judged. Consider what happens when I ask people to give me feedback on workshops I conduct.

Because I want to continually improve the training I do, I use evaluation forms to collect feedback. Usually I end up learning more about the people filling out the evaluation than I do about the training.

"The session was too long," one person will respond. Another will say, "I'd like to see this spread out over more time." One participant will remark the room was too hot. Another will comment it was too cold. Some people like the slide presentation and dislike working in groups. Others say the slides were boring, but group work was great. In each case, people are saying more about themselves than they are about the workshop.

I've received a variety of reactions about me from people who have attended my trainings and university courses. Generally, people like me although some have not. I've been judged as humorous, intelligent, boring, flexible, rigid, excellent, average, folksy, opinionated, and encouraging. Why is it that there are so many different judgments when there is only one person being judged?

There are different judgments because each person interprets the events of her life through a unique filtering system. We all see through our own filters which are composed of the sum total of all our previous programming. Each person's mind contains different beliefs, thoughts, words, values and experiences. And since we filter what we see through our minds, we each create a unique interpretation.

Because each workshop participant sees me through a different set of filters, each makes a unique interpretation. Some participants see me as helpful. Others see me as an obstacle. Some notice my willingness to share. Some people hear my humor and others wonder why people are laughing.

Since everyone perceives me differently, how a person sees me tells about them than it does about me. If someone judges me as boring, that tells about her programming, her beliefs and her values. It also indicates that she is choosing to bore herself with me. Her interpretation of me reveals plenty about her. It tells little about me.

Likewise, if someone judges me as entertaining, that tells about his programming, beliefs and values. That interpretation reveals that he is choosing to entertain himself with me. Again, it's about him, and not about me.

Also, if I judge others, that judgment is about me. If I judge a workshop participant as lazy, I reveal more about how I choose to experience the participant than I do about the person himself. I tell about my beliefs, my values and my programming.

Judgments are never about the thing or the person being judged. Judgments are always about the judges.

"Tell it like it is" is a phrase made popular by Howard Cosell. He uses it to justify a judgmental mindset and convince his audience that being critical is a form of honesty worthy of respect.

Actually, there is no such thing as telling it like it is. There is only telling it the way I see it or telling it the way you see it. Howard Cosell tells it the way he sees it. He shares his judgments, his interpretations, his views. However, his judgments are not the way it is. His judgments are simply his judgments. And like any other judger, his comments tell more about Howard Cosell than they do about the object or person being judged.

The Payoffs

We don't judge solely because we've been trained to do so. We judge because we get something back. There is something in it for us. There are payoffs.

Being Right

One payoff we get from judging is that of being right. It is a reward we get from judging and it helps to perpetuate our evaluative thinking.

When we judge someone as lazy, and then notice their lazy acts, we prove we are right. When we label an experience as excellent and get others to agree with us, we are right. When we blame our boss for his stupidity, and the project fails, we are right again.

Judging helps us to be right. And when we confirm our rightness, we feel good about ourselves. Being right is a way we have of proving our worth to ourselves. And while the shot of self-worth we get from being right may feel good for the moment, we pay a heavy price for its existence.

Being Right Doesn't Work

In the first place, being right doesn't work. I'm reminded of the cartoon I saw that showed a patient in a hospital bed bandaged from head to toe with both legs and arms in traction. The doctor stood near the bed looking at her clipboard. The words spoken by the patient were, "But I had the right of way!"

Did being right prevent the accident? No. Did being right eliminate pain and suffering? No. Did being right work in this case? Absolutely not!

You can judge your spouse as lazy. And by concentrating on all the things he does that prove your judgment to yourself you can be right. So what's so valuable about being right? Did being right help encourage your spouse to generate more energy and enthusiasm? Did being right create more harmony in the relationship? Did being right help you feel more loving towards your spouse?

Perhaps you don't like the vacation spot your wife picked out and you judge it as boring. You can be right. You can prove to yourself every day that the vacation site is a boring place for you to be. So what? Does being right help you enjoy your vacation? Does it help you experience relaxation or excitement? Does it get you anything at all other than the satisfaction of being right? Of course not.

Alienation

Another reason being right doesn't work is because it alienates us from others. When we set it up so that we are right and others are wrong, we concentrate on differences rather than commonalities. Being right promotes a "me vs. them" attitude. That attitude creates mental separation which puts distance between us and other people.

Being right sabotages cooperation and feelings of togetherness. It is difficult to be right and cooperate simultaneously. Cooperation and togetherness result from a "me *and* them" approach to life. "Me *vs.* them" thinking interferes with reaching consensus and the cooperative process.

When we believe in and act out a "me vs. them" orientation, we put ourselves in a state of conflict. Constant judging, comparing and proving creates inner turmoil and anxiety. Fatigue and exhaustion result from chasing around proving our judgments to ourselves. The physical and emotional energy we use judging could more effectively be directed towards problem-solving, building a relationship, or fostering cooperation and feelings of mutuality.

Perspective

There is a third reason why being right doesn't work. When we focus on making ourselves right and others wrong, we lose perspective. We tend to concentrate on specific incidents that back up our judgments and ignore those that don't. In our rush to judge and be right, we fail to see the total picture. And the picture we do see is distorted by our desire to be right.

Better Than

Being "better than" is another payoff we get from judging. Judging breeds comparison and comparison leads to one upsman-ship. If I judge you as average, and me as excellent, then I get to be "better than." If I judge her as messy and myself as neat, then I'm "better than."

Being "better than" is another tool for injecting a shot of self-worth into a person with low self-esteem. If you don't feel good about yourself, you can chop someone else down with judgments and raise yourself by comparison. Maybe you still don't feel totally good, but you can take some comfort in seeing the other person worse than you.

This strategy is not one we use consciously or with forethought. We don't say to ourselves, "O.K., I want to feel better about myself so I'll judge Jack as ugly and then I'll be better than him." The effect though, is the same as if we'd done it on purpose. It helps us feel good temporarily and keeps us caught in the judgment trap.

When you notice you're generating a "better than" mentality, use it as a clue. Ask yourself, "What am I creating in my life that results in such low self-esteem that I want to be better than?" A more beneficial use of your time and energy would be to take steps to raise your own esteem without placing people below you through the use of judgments.

I'm Being Judged

Have you ever been around a judgmental person? Did you wonder what he was thinking about you? Did you wonder what he said to others after you left?

Another price you pay for judging others is fear that others are judging you. Because you judge, you tend to believe others do it too. If you've developed a belief that others are judging you, it's most likely because you frequently judge them.

Your words are like a boomerang. They come back to you. If you send out acceptance, you receive acceptance in return. If you send out judgments, you get judged. By reducing your judgments of others and turning off your evaluator for long periods of time, you will stop worrying if and how others are evaluating you.

Put-Downs

Desire to achieve a "better than" view of self has led to the ritualization of the PUT-DOWN. The put-down is a quick one liner intended to drop the other person to a level below you. Examples include:

"Nice going, Stupid,"

"What a klutz."

"She's uglier than a duck."

Put-downs with a sarcastic flavor are currently popular and attempt to hide the judgment with a ring of humor.

"I don't see how he can walk and chew gum at the same time."

I'm not sure she was there when they passed out all the parts."

"If she had half a brain, she'd be dangerous."

The put-down does exactly what it says it does. It puts the other person down, thereby raising you in comparison.

The put-down is a clue of low self-esteem and a desire to dominate. If you hear yourself using put-downs, stop and question, "Why am I trying to raise myself by putting someone else down? What is it I'm saying about myself by using put-downs?"

"We're Just Kidding"

Occasionally before one of my workshops, I will overhear colleagues having fun by putting each other down. Around the registration table and over coffee, they will jab at each other with remarks like:

"I see you got here all right. Did your mother wake you up?"

"Look out, Klutz, or you'll spill the coffee."

"Hey, can't you even spell your name right?"

This fun-poking way to begin the morning seems friendly enough at first glance. Beneath this "affectionate name-calling," however, is a serious situation that is harmful to the judger and the judgee alike.

Put-downs of any nature are destructive. There is no such thing as affectionate name-calling. What is said in supposed jest is simply a poorly veiled attempt to put another person down. Each statement contains a bit of truth recognized by both the sender and the receiver.

The judger is harmed because she perpetuates her judgmental mindset that keeps her stuck in evaluative thinking. The judgee is harmed because the subconscious mind does not take a joke. The subconscious mind simply records what is spoken or thought. It doesn't filter out put-downs that were meant as jokes from those that weren't. The impression is recorded regardless of its intention.

Put-downs are an opportunity for you to take a step away from the judgment trap and take one towards the language of acceptance. When you hear your put-downs or catch them forming in your mind, stop. As an alternative, give the intended recipient of your verbal jab a compliment. Tell them you're glad they are here this morning or that you look forward to working with them today. Share an appreciation. Tell them about something they did that has a positive effect on your life. Or simply remain silent. Resist the temptation to put others down aloud or even silently to yourself.

THE BLAME GAME

One indication at being caught in the Judgment Trap is blame. When you hear yourself blaming or finding fault, you can be assured you are still keeping yourself stuck in the grip of the judgment trap. Some examples follow:

"It's my parents' fault. They were too permissive when I was young."

"My teachers never made me learn the basics. They're to blame for my poor spelling."

"It's my boss' fault we didn't get the contract. He wasn't prepared for the presentation."

Blame is an example of programming that helps you think and behave unself-responsibly. It's a way of using language to assign responsibility to someone or something else for the conditions that exist in your life.

To blame is to give up personal power. If you blame your parents, your boss, your friends, or anyone else for your problems, you leave them in control. You give them the power, render yourself impotent and leave yourself out of control.

When you blame, you program your mind to focus on others. That keeps you from looking at the role you play in a given situation and keeps responsibility off your back.

Blaming also prevents you from taking control and moving effectively to alter the situation. It uses up time and energy that could be used to take a look at why you are blaming in the first place or on how you could positively affect the situation. Blaming exhausts your present moments and keeps you from implementing corrective action.

Imagine your child bursting through your front door to tell you his sister has been hit by a car in front of your home. You rush to the scene and find her with a broken leg, cuts, scratches, and assorted bruises. Would you take the time to find out whose fault it was? Would you immediately blame those who you determine responsible after collecting several versions of the accident? Hardly.

Chances are, you would immediately assess the problem and search for solutions. You would take action, probably by calling an ambulance, helping your child get comfortable, and covering her with a blanket. You would expend your efforts helping her stay calm and relaxed.

Any time spent fixing blame, in your mind or aloud, would detract from your efforts to take helpful action. Any seconds you spent thinking about who was at fault would be seconds that delayed implementing solutions.

Blame and fault finding serve no useful purpose in an emergency. And they serve no useful purpose in our everyday lives, either.

Blaming my boss for messing up the presentation does nothing to improve it for next time. Blaming the post office for slow delivery keeps me from looking at what I can do to make sure the package gets there on time in the future. Blaming my son for not filling up the car with gas prevents me from finding a workable solution so that the situation doesn't reoccur.

Blaming is finger pointing. It's an attempt to put the finger on someone or something else. When you hear yourself using words that blame, imagine that you are pointing your index finger at the object you believe is at fault. Then take a quick look at where your other fingers are pointing.

Once you determine where those other fingers are pointing, start there. Ask yourself, "What role did I play in this drama?" or "What did I do to help perpetuate this situation?" Instead of blaming and programming your mind to look to others to find fault, use your time and energy in self-examination or to search for solutions. Not only will you be taking a positive step that could well prove beneficial to the specific situation, you will also be reprogramming your mind to think action instead of blame. You will be moving one step closer to freeing yourself from the judgment trap.

Self-Judgment

One danger inherent in using judgmental language is the tendency of those who judge others to judge themselves.

"I'm not as good looking as Harry."

"Maxine makes twice the money I do."

"I always beat Sarah in racquetball. I'm better than she is."

Comparing yourself with others flows out of a belief that you should be comparable and that you should measure up. The belief is you should be more, you should be better, you should be like someone else.

Judging yourself against another person's norm is a quick way to produce feelings of inferiority. When you judge yourself by someone else's standard, you can never be enough. There is always someone you can find who is richer, healthier, stronger, or more attractive than you.

Certainly it is reasonable to admire others, to value the positive personality traits they possess and the useful abilities they have developed. The problem doesn't occur because of admiration. It occurs when you get down on yourself because you don't measure up. It occurs because when you don't feel "enough," you deprive yourself and the universe of a full you.

Step out of this section of the judgment trap by developing an internal standard. Determine what is acceptable for you and work to achieve it. Eliminate language that compares and the feelings of inferiority and distance it produces.

SELF-CRITICISM

Self-criticism is another way to injure yourself when caught in the judgment trap. It's possible to beat yourself unmercifully with self-depreciating words that label and criticize your appearance, performance, and/or achievements. Self-criticism takes several forms. They include the second guess, self put-downs, using adjectives to describe yourself, and the "only/just" depreciation.

Second Guessing

The second guess is recognizable because it often begins with the words "I should have . . ." or "I shouldn't have . . ."

"I should have rejected the transfer."

"Maybe I shouldn't have told him what I felt about that issue."

"I should have apologized."

This form of self-criticism can debilitate you no matter what alternatives you choose in a given situation. If you choose A, you can get after yourself for not choosing B. If you choose B, you can get after yourself for not choosing A. When you second guess, you keep yourself from putting full energy into the path you do choose. You deprive yourself of making a full effort with either choice.

Self Put-Downs

Self put-downs are another distinctive form of self-criticism.

"I'm so uncoordinated."

"What a jerk I am!"

"How silly of me!"

These and other self-rejecting words and phrases are harmful because they affect how you behave. The words you use to describe yourself create or strengthen the ways you view yourself. How you choose to view yourself determines what you believe about yourself. What you choose to believe about yourself shapes how you choose to act in the future.

Certainly there are times when you make a decision that doesn't turn out the way you had hoped it would. That doesn't make you stupid. You can only make yourself stupid with the words you choose to use and the thoughts you choose to think about the decision you made.

Of course there are occasions when you fail to accomplish a goal or complete a task. That doesn't make you a failure. It only makes you a person who didn't accomplish a goal or complete the task yet. You only become a failure through your choice of words and how you decide to think about yourself.

Stop programming yourself with self-rejecting words and phrases. Don't call yourself klutzy, boring, or stupid. It's okay to feel like a klutz on occasion and it's important to stop talking about it as if it were an integral part of your being. Refrain from sending messages to yourself as if that's "just the way you are."

Recently I enjoyed eating out with a friend. We shared a plate of nachos stacked high with cheese, tomatoes, peppers, and onions. Both of us had trouble negotiating the distance between the plate of nachos and our mouths without spilling portions of our dinner.

As my friend surveyed the messy tablecloth in front of her, she remarked, "I'm such a slob." After a moment's reflection, she rephrased her thought. "No," she said, "I'm just being a little messy tonight."

What a difference in her words! "I'm such a slob," labels my friend as "that way." That choice of language equates her with being a slob and sets in motion forces that help her to see herself as a slob. "I'm being a little messy tonight," simply describes the situation. It does not brand her as "that way," and recognizes there are many times when she is not messy.

Describing You
Versus Describing Behavior

One way to step out of the judgment trap is to do as my friend did and change language that describes you as "that way" to language that describes your behavior.

Describes You	*Describes Behavior*
I am not intelligent.	I behaved unintelligently.
I'm silly.	I acted silly.
I am thoughtless.	That was a thoughtless act.
I'm no fun.	I wasn't fun to be with last night.

I am not honest.	I behaved in a dishonest way.
I'm a liar.	I lied that time.

Reread the above examples aloud. Feel the difference? Imagine the effect that each style of communication has on your subconscious mind. Which kind of programming do you want filling your bio-computer?

Only/Just

One stylized form of the self put-down is the "only/just" depreciation.

"I'm just a housewife."
"I'm only a teacher."
"I'm just a teenager."
"I'm only a friend."
"I'm just a junior executive."
"I'm only on the second team."

Use of the words "only" or "just" imply that what you are is not enough and that you should be more. Choice of "only/just" language diminishes what you are in your own eyes and in your own mind. "Only" and "just" shout out your inadequacies and remind yourself and others that you're not very special.

Drop "only" and "just" from your language patterns. When you catch yourself using them to put yourself down, stop and rephrase the sentence eliminating those words. State proudly, "I'm a housewife," or "I'm a teacher."

Self-Criticism and Motivation

Do you believe you'll be a happier, more successful person if you blame, judge, and criticize yourself? Do you think put-downs are an effective way to kick yourself into high gear? Do you believe you'll get more accomplished if you get after yourself? Do you think that self-criticism is an expedient path to meaningful change?

Sorry. It doesn't work that way.

Self-rejection is a way to immobilize yourself. Anyone busy getting after himself is not busy changing, taking constructive action or searching for positive solutions.

"But I motivate myself with criticism," a friend once told me. "When I see myself as stupid, I get mad and want to do something about it. If I think of myself as lazy, that helps me to get going because I don't like to be lazy."

Certainly it's possible to get some short term results with self-criticism. Beating yourself up with negative words may be the catalyst for finishing your report. Calling yourself lazy can serve as the impetus to get the garage cleaned. Prodding yourself with the self-rejecting phrases of "chicken" or "scaredy cat" may enable you to ask someone for a date.

So what? What for? And who wants it? It is possible to finish the report without berating yourself. Cleaning the garage is do-able minus self put-downs. And asking someone for a date can be done without psyching yourself up with self-depreciation.

Even if it were true that you need self-criticism to motivate yourself, what you gain is not worth what you lose. You gain a completed report and you diminish your self-esteem. You gain a clean garage and you lose a piece of your self-worth. You gain an opportunity for a date and lose by weakening your image of yourself.

Finishing a report, cleaning the garage, and getting a date are important. They are not, however, as important as how you choose to think about yourself. Your thoughts become your beliefs, which contribute to how you see yourself. And your self-image has a greater impact on your life than whether or not you complete a task.

Self-criticism often creates less motivation. Instead of producing action that results in a complete report, it helps create depression which often breeds inaction. And the report remains unfinished. And the derogatory remarks to self, discourage rather than encourage cleaning the garage. Likewise, self put-downs promote fear rather than the desired confidence necessary to ask for a date.

Getting after yourself with criticism serves no useful purpose. It wastes time. It uses up energy. It lowers self-esteem, and it keeps you from concentrating on change, growth, or improving unsatisfying conditions. Constructive change made after self-criticism is done in spite of that criticism, not because of it.

Don't misinterpret here. I am not arguing against taking an honest look at yourself through self-assessment. Self-assessment is an important step in the change process and feedback is useful for giving yourself necessary information when contemplating a new direction.

When you do want to change, constructive feedback is useful and helpful. Self-criticism is not. And there is a difference.

Constructive Feedback and Self-Criticism

Constructive feedback differs from self-criticism in that it describes the situation rather than evaluates it. The difference can be explained by examining what goes on when a friend and I play racquetball.

My friend constantly evaluates his shots, his efforts, and his performance. When he is scoring points and putting the ball where he wants it, he engages in self-talk that is evaluative. He thinks, "good shot," "nice going," and "great effort." Likewise, when his game is not what he would like it to be, he continues to evaluate. He uses self-critical programming like "stupid shot," "dumb idea," and "terrible backhand." Many times his self-depreciation is loud, angry, and accompanied by strong feeling.

When my racquetball opponent begins to get after himself with evaluative thoughts and self-critical outbursts, I know his chances of playing well or winning are diminished. Now it is two against one. Because of his self-talk, my friend now has two opponents, me and himself. As expected, as soon as he starts the self-criticism, his game deteriorates rapidly.

My approach differs from that of my evaluative opponent. Instead of using self-criticism, I find it useful to give myself constructive feedback. I simply describe in non-evaluative terms what I see.

Instead of judging my shot as "awful," I notice that it wasn't low enough to be a winner. Instead of evaluating my backhand as "terrible," I notice that I wasn't in a position to get full strength behind it. As an alternative to criticizing my strategy of using ceiling shots as "stupid," I give myself the feedback that my opponent is returning all my ceiling shots with confidence and strength.

I notice what I do, where my shots go, and what happens as a result. I put that feedback into my computer-like brain and trust that without the self-interference of self-critical evaluations my mind and body will work efficiently to make the necessary adjustments.

When I catch myself evaluating a shot as "stupid" or "terrible," I stop and change my thought. I rephrase my self-talk so that it gives me useful information. "I was out of position," is useful. "Stupid" is not. "I hit it softer than I wanted to," is useful. "Dumb shot" is not. Clearly, constructive feedback is more helpful than self-criticism.

Characteristics of Constructive Feedback

Constructive feedback embodies three main characteristics. It is specific, focuses on behavior, and relates information. Look over the next two sentences and determine which fit the characteristics of constructive feedback.

A) "I was rude to her yesterday."

B) "I called her 'silly' yesterday and hung up on her."

The first sentence is an example of self-criticism. Rude is the key word here. What is rude anyway? Rude is general and focuses on you as a person rather than on your behavior. Constructive feedback would contain specific information. It would describe a specific behavior like the sentences that follow:

"I interrupted her sentence three times."

"I called her ugly."

"I stuck out my tongue at her."

The second example is constructive feedback. "I called her 'silly' yesterday and hung up on her," describes my exact behavior. It tells me what I did and gives me the information necessary to decide whether or not I like the behavior.

Now see if you can accurately pick the constructive feedback examples from the sentences which follow. Make a mental mark in your mind as to which are examples of constructive feedback and which are self-criticizing.

1. I'm irresponsible

2. I arrived at the meeting after it started.

3. I didn't do a very good job.

4. The last time I played golf, I lost 4 balls and scored 116.

5. I'm 16 pounds heavier than I'd like to be.
6. I'm a terrible driver on icy roads.
7. I lost $50 in the poker game last night.
8. I'm slow with math.

Answers

1. Self-criticism. Irresponsible is a judgment because it's general. What specific behavior was it that you did? What is it exactly that you're judging as irresponsible?

2. Constructive feedback. No judgment here. Arriving after the meeting started is not good or bad. It's just arriving after the meeting started. You have given yourself useful information.

3. Self-criticism. Good is judgmental. What was it about the job you did that you're rating as not good? It could have been messy, incomplete, late, inaccurate, plagiarized, or all of the above. "Not very good," does not give you useful information.

4. Constructive feedback. This statement gives you information about your performance. It doesn't make you a good or a bad person. It lets you be a person who lost 4 balls and scored 116 last time.

5. Constructive feedback. Being 16 pounds heavier doesn't make you fat or ugly. It only makes you 16 pounds heavier. It is specific and gives you accurate feedback you can use in determining whether or not to do anything about those 16 pounds.

6. Self-criticism. So what is terrible? Is it that you skidded into a ditch, got sweaty palms, had an accident, or just didn't act confidently? Until you get clear about what terrible is, you've not given yourself any helpful data.

7. Constructive feedback. This statement concentrates on what happened. It is specific and non-judgmental.

8. Self-criticism. In addition to being evaluative, this statement has a ring of "That's just the way I am." It focuses on the person rather than the behavior.

Self-Change

Self-critical language and judgmental thoughts get in the way of effective change. A person caught up in getting after herself is not focusing on constructive solutions. A person mired in self-criticism has little desire to move forward. And a person who has chipped away at her own self-esteem through the use of repetitious self-blame is not forming a solid base from which to attempt change.

Change flows best from self-acceptance. If you don't have it, you are not as likely to risk and grow. You'll be too busy trying to prove yourself right or defend yourself against the imagined attacks of others.

Constantly being in the midst of evaluating yourself is not the most helpful place from which to attempt self-growth. Without self-acceptance you will lack support as you risk and attempt to move out of your comfort zone. To increase your self-acceptance, talk sense to yourself by increasing your use of descriptive feedback.

Fault Finding

Finding fault is looking for weakness. Since we always find what we look for, it makes more sense to look for strengths. And it's just as easy to look for and find strength as it is to notice weakness. Every time you catch yourself finding fault, *stop* and look for something to praise or appreciate. For each fault, list three strengths or three things you appreciate. If you're not in a convenient spot to write them, say them silently to yourself.

Complaints

Words of complaint are a waste of time. Instead of complaining, think of one thing you can do to help improve the situation. Then do it. If you don't think of any, don't strengthen the situation by adding the negative energy of complaining.

Labels

Beware of labels other than those on jelly jars and prescription drugs. If you label yourself as uncreative, you become even less able to create.

When you catch yourself labeling yourself with "I am" statements as detailed in Chapter Four, change the labels to words that describe your behavior.

- Say "I'm not creating much" rather than "I'm not creative."
- Use "I've forgotten my keys" instead of "I'm forgetful."

It's also helpful, when changing labels to descriptions, to add the words, "this time" or "today." By saying "I'm not creating much *today,*" you remind (and re-mind) yourself that the uncreativity you are experiencing is only temporary. "I've forgotten my keys *this time*" does not send yourself the message that you are a forgetful person. It merely describes a one-time phenomenon that may or may not happen again.

Labeling others is a variation of the judgment trap and can also be altered by using the language of acceptance. Labeling another person as dumb, dishonest, boring, or unhelpful narrows them in your mind. By using a one-word description of a person, you take all of their characteristics, abilities, attitudes, and personality traits and squeeze them into one concept. You then tend to see that person as that label.

No characteristic, no ability, personality trait, or attitude exists in pure form. All of us are a mixture. We are part honest and part dishonest, part intelligent and part not so intelligent. We are helpful and unhelpful, coordinated and uncoordinated, all at the same time.

One alternative to labeling others is to describe what you see going on. "She added her score incorrectly" is a description. "She is a cheater" is a label. "He withheld important information" describes, while "He lied" labels.

Positive Labels

What about positive labels, like gifted and athletic? Aren't they okay?

A label is a label is a label. All labels are confining. They categorize and pigeonhole. Being seen as athletic is as limiting as being seen as non-athletic. Seeing yourself as a brain can be as destructive as seeing yourself as unintelligent.

It's not so much what "positive" labels allow you to see as it is what they help you ignore. By labeling a person as athletic, you see his athletic ability and are more likely to miss those attributes that are not athletic or that show other abilities. When you attach a gifted label to someone, you put her in a box that's difficult to escape.

Another danger in using "positive" labels is that it maintains the habit of labeling. By using "positive" labels, you continue to judge and communicate to yourself that judging is acceptable. You solidify yourself in the judgment trap.

People in Progress

Another technique for escaping the judgment trap is to view yourself and others as people in progress. None of us is complete. We are all unfinished, moving toward realization of our full potential.

"Yet," "so far," and "at this time" are useful words that will help you remember we are all people in progress. They are an integral part of the language of acceptance.

"I'm not as successful as I'd like to be in math *yet*," is more accepting of yourself than, "I'm not as successful as I'd like to be in math."

"*At this time*, she doesn't type well," is not as final as, "She doesn't type well."

"He hasn't learned it *so far*," is more likely to help you see him as a person in progress than, "He hasn't learned it."

Practice using "yet," "so far," and "at this time" when you think or talk about yourself and others. It will help you to be more accepting of what is, prevent you from labeling, and increase the chance that growth will occur.

Gossip

Stay away from gossip sessions. You won't find the language of acceptance there. Did you ever hear constructive gossip? Or gossip that focused on solutions? Probably not.

Gossip is destructive. It is full of put-downs, rumors, interpretations, and judgment. It is divisive, separating, and nonproductive.

Gossip does serve one useful function. It is the final test. If you can exist in a room full of people who are engaged in gossip that judges and puts others down without joining in or without judging the judging, you have passed the test. You are free of the judgment trap.

PRAISE & CRITICISM

Steering clear of the judgment trap also involves learning how to praise and criticize in ways consistent with the language of acceptance. Let's examine praise first.

Praise is the number one behavior modification tool employed by teachers, parents and managers alike. Its use has been advocated by teacher trainers, child rearing experts, and management consultants throughout the country. Praise has been praised by many who believe it is healthy, worthwhile, and effective.

Teachers tell me praise builds self-esteem and motivates students. Parents tell me praise helps them to get their children to do what they want them to do. Employees tell me they would like to hear more praise for their efforts.

The assumption is that praise is good. Yet what if it isn't so? What if praise is unhelpful, unhealthy, or destructive? What if praise manipulates, evaluates, and places you securely in the grasp of the judgment trap? Let's take a closer look.

There are three types of praise; evaluative, descriptive, and appreciative. Each gets its name from the function it performs.

Evaluative praise evaluates, descriptive praise describes, and appreciative praise appreciates. Each has a different impact on its recipient.

Evaluative Praise

Examples of evaluative praise include:
"You're a *good* boy."
"You did a *great* job.'"
"That's a *beautiful* picture."

When you praise someone with evaluative praise, you rate them with words like good, excellent, fantastic, super, far-out, wonderful, and tremendous. In each case your words represent a judgment of what you think about the other person. Your praise is a judgmental interpretation of their behavior, accomplishments, ideas, appearance or character.

Evaluative praise helps the person being praised to feel good temporarily. In that sense, evaluative praise works very much like a drug. It helps people feel good for the moment and allows them to get hooked. Children are especially susceptible to the dependency induced by heavy doses of evaluative praise.

An art teacher once shared her frustration with me, explaining how she tried to wean praise-dependent children off evaluative praise. A child would finish a project, bring it to her and participate in the following discussion:

Child: How do you like my picture? Is it good?

Teacher: I enjoy the way you've filled the whole paper with color.

Child: But is it good?

Teacher: I notice you've used seven different colors.

Child: But do you think it's good?

Teacher: Tell me what you think about it.

Child: I like it, but I want to know if it's good.

The above conversation was not atypical. It happened continually in this teacher's art room, initiated by students who were hooked on evaluative praise and looking for a quick fix.

These students and others like them have learned to depend on others for their measures of success. They have come to see others as the major source of approval in their lives. And they have come to "need" a regular shot of evaluative praise to maintain their sense of self-worth.

This phenomenon is not confined to children. Many adults spend energy and time chasing approval. What they want is for others to evaluate them positively, to tell them they are good, excellent, beautiful or wonderful. Without these constant reminders, these evaluative praise-dependent people aren't sure of their own worth.

Excessive use of evaluative praise teaches people to look away from themselves for evidence of their worth. They become "externals" and rely on proof from others for feelings of importance. They do not develop an adequate internal standard and do not trust their own interpretations of their worth. Evaluative praise encourages people to take their self-image from others' perceptions and to depend on that.

Two Parts of Praise

There are two parts of praise. The first part is what is said. The second part is what the person praised says to herself after she's been praised. And it's what the person says to herself about the praise that has the most beneficial effect on self-esteem, worth and feelings of personal power. Both appreciative and descriptive praise help to build that strong internal view of self.

For example, let's say my children have cleaned the garage. If I want to praise them, I have several choices. I can use evaluative praise such as, "What a great job of cleaning the garage," or "You sure were good workers."

I'm not going to choose evaluative praise. I don't want my children seeing me as the source of their self-worth. I want that to come from within them. I want them to develop strong internal feelings of worth and self-esteem. To facilitate that, I will choose words of praise that let them say to themselves, "I did a great job," or "I'm a good worker." That's where appreciative and descriptive praise are most helpful.

Appreciative Praise

Appreciative praise appreciates. When I praise appreciatively, I simply share my appreciation. My words might be, "I was happy to seen the clean garage and realize I could choose to do something else this afternoon. I really appreciate your efforts. Thanks."

Notice I didn't judge or evaluate their efforts, their motivation or the results. I simply shared what I appreciated. That left them free to make the evaluation. The rating comes from within. My children could say to themselves, "We did a good job."

When using appreciative praise, it is important to focus comments on specific acts. Do not praise by labeling character traits like trustworthy, dependable and honest. Saying, "I appreciate your dependability," is simply another way to evaluate a person. A comment like, "I appreciate you being here exactly when you said you would," allows the other person to say to herself, "I am dependable."

Descriptive Praise

Descriptive praise also helps the speaker stay clear of the evaluative mode and creates space for the receiver to make that determination himself. Descriptive praise describes. It is used to describe what is seen or heard. It speaks to accomplishments or states the situation. Examples follow:

"There must have been close to 10,000 leaves in the yard when you began. Now I only see three or four."

"Your report listed every fact I wanted. It helped me understand the problem."

"I could see my face clearly in those plates you washed."

Notice the absence of evaluation in descriptive praise. You won't find, "You did a good job cleaning up the yard," "That was a beautiful report," or "You are an excellent dishwasher." Choosing words that describe the situation lets the person hearing the description draw his own conclusion. Again, the evaluation comes from him.

Manipulation and Self-Responsibility

Evaluative praise is often an effort to control, to manipulate, and to be in charge of another person. The outward appearance of praise like "good girl," "excellent behavior," and "very good meal" is that I want to say something nice to you. The ulterior motive is to get you to be more like I'd like you to be. I tell you you're good when you're quiet so I can manipulate you into being quiet more often. I tell you that you look beautiful with long hair, so you'll continue to wear your hair the way *I* like it. Evaluative praise is an unself-responsible way to communicate because it's an attempt to be responsible for more than oneself.

What's So Good About Good?

Another characteristic of evaluative praise is that it does not provide useful information. I first realized this the day I opened my daughter's third grade report card.

"Marti is a good speller," it said. So what does that mean? What is a "good speller"? Is her spelling good on everyday assignments or only after she studies words for a week? Does she spell twenty words correctly each week or thirty? I didn't know.

What exactly did "good speller" tell me? Not much. I didn't know which words Marti could spell or where she experienced difficulty. I didn't know if Marti was a good speller to begin with and had failed to improve, or if she started out as a poor speller and was now learning at an accelerated pace. All I knew was that her teacher evaluated her spelling as "good." Not much useful information there for a father who cares about his daughter's schoolwork.

Later that week a colleague told me he had read the article I wrote for our company newsletter. He said, "It sure was good." Again, I was left with little information. What does "good" mean? I didn't know if he found a useful idea, felt my article would help promote our shared objectives, or enjoyed hearing one of my life's experiences. I didn't know whether he thought it was humorous, helpful, or grammatically correct. I only know he thought it was good.

I haven't always questioned the value of evaluative praise. There was a time in my life when I enjoyed it. My self-esteem was low and I openly chased external proof of my worth. During that period I loved hearing "beautiful," "good," "excellent," and similar evaluations. It was not uncommon for me at that stage in my development to spend a weekend working in my darkroom. The following week I would eagerly show my photos to any one who would sit still long enough to view them. My aim was to hear oohs and ahhs. I wanted approval. I wanted praise. And I wanted that praise in the form of positive evaluation.

Today I operate on a different plateau in terms of my self-esteem. I no longer want others to be my measure of success. I have developed an internal standard for my work and for my life. I know when my photography is "good." And I know when it isn't. The evaluations of others are no longer necessary or helpful to me.

Don't get me wrong. I love praise and I want it. And the praise I find most useful and enhancing to my self-esteem is appreciative and descriptive. I thoroughly enjoy it when a participant tells how he used information gained at my workshop to reach a personal goal. I choose to be excited when a colleague shares her appreciation at my listening to her talk out a serious problem. I like it when I get a note in the mail informing me that my cassette tape presentation helped the purchaser to look at a concern from a new perspective. Yes, I enjoy praise. And I find it more useful and informative when that praise is descriptive or appreciative.

What kind of praise do you like to hear? Do you prefer your supervisor to say, "That was a good report," or "I found your report clear and to the point. It helped me understand both sides of that issue"? Would you rather hear your spouse remark, "You sure are a good listener," or "I enjoy the way you listen to me and hear me out. I like knowing I can express my anger without you taking it personally. I appreciate the time you give to hearing my concerns. Thanks"?

Regardless of the style of praise you prefer, appreciative and descriptive praise are the most self-responsible. When you praise in those ways, you assume a non-manipulative stance. Your message is more direct and concentrates on relaying information about you, the sender. Structuring your praise with appreciative and descriptive language lets the receiver assume responsibility for interpreting the information. You step out of the role of judge and allow the other person to choose their own evaluation.

Changing Your Praise

Moving from evaluative to appreciative and descriptive praise is another strategy for avoiding the judgment trap. It's a way of neutralizing your internal evaluator and moving increasingly towards the language of acceptance.

Begin by noticing praise. Listen to the praise you receive this week. Categorize it. Record it in your journal.

If you find you're getting an abundance of evaluative praise, ask people to explain what they mean. When someone says, "What an excellent dinner," ask them what they mean by excellent. If someone evaluates your report, cross-stitch, or presentation as "good," ask them, "What do you like about it?" Find out what people really mean by fine, super, fantastic, beautiful, and tremendous.

Also, notice when you use evaluative praise. Train your mind to hear your own "goods" and "excellents." Then ask yourself what *you* really mean by that. When you decide, share it with the other person using descriptive and appreciative language.

Praise Practice

To develop the habit of using non-judgmental praise, it is necessary to practice. Begin by setting aside five minutes each day as practice time. I suggest you use a specific time either first thing in the morning, right before you go to bed or whenever you can consistently free up five minutes for this activity.

Begin with yourself. For the first few days use that five minutes to praise yourself. Each day write three sentence completions to the following sentence starter:

I appreciate the way I . . . _____

_____

_____

Examples include:
"I appreciate the way I say hello to everyone in the morning."
I appreciate the way I consistently use this five minutes to practice praise."
"I appreciate the way I keep my word to others."

Next, describe three situations, accomplishments, acts or circumstances you were involved in that you feel deserve self-praise. Be sure to be *descriptive*. Write them out.

Examples include:
"I completed five items on my 'to do' list today, reorganized my filing system, and started on the final report."
"I read over 250 pages in the manual on business finance."
"I gave Robert one hour of my time and listened while he worked through a problem he was having."

Upon conclusion of writing each item, take time to feel the positive effects. Say each one aloud and then notice the positive feeling spread throughout your body. Enjoy.

When you feel skilled at designing appreciative and descriptive statements about yourself, move on to others. During that five-minute practice session, design appreciative and descriptive comments to share with others throughout the day.

Think of people who shared their time, gave you support or helped you out in one way or another. Remember colleagues or family members who model honesty, persistence or other characteristics you admire. Or think of a time when you noticed someone doing something well. Practice by writing an appreciative or descriptive comment that lets them know what you observed.

Practice using one or more of the following sentence starters:

I appreciate it when . . .

I enjoy your . . .

I like the way you . . .

In each case, make sure your written comments are specific and descriptive. Keep them free of evaluation. When you have your statement the way you want it, give it to the other person. Send them a note or tell them face to face. Then praise yourself (non-evaluatively) for your growing skill of designing appreciative and descriptive praise.

Criticism

Criticism and praise are closely related. They are flip sides of the same coin. Criticism, like praise, can be delievered in evaluative, descriptive or unappreciative terms.

Terrible, ordinary, ugly, sloppy, poor, disgusting, and awful are examples of criticism that evaluates. These evaluative words, like their cousins, good, excellent, and beautiful, give very little useful information. It's of little benefit to know the report was terrible unless I know specifically what was terrible about it. It's of no use to hear the article I wrote was disgusting unless I know what it was the person who criticized it chose to be disgusted about.

Tell me the report was inaccurate in three places or that it failed to cover a certain part of the topic and you give me information I can use to strengthen my report for next time. Tell me you didn't like how much I used four-letter words in my article, and I gain some insight into why you thought it was disgusting. Criticize me in descriptive language and I have some valuable data to consider. Or use evaluative criticism and leave me wondering what it was you thought was terrible, disgusting or awful.

Sharing a lack of appreciation is another way to give people specific feedback to consider. Examples include:

"I didn't like cleaning up the sink before I began dinner."

"I don't appreciate it when you start the meeting fifteen minutes late."

"I like it best when you leave the bathroom the way you found it before you took your shower. I don't appreciate picking up towels and finding a wet floor."

People generally respond better when I share what I don't appreciate or describe what I don't like, than they do if I criticize with evaluation. I get a quicker response by stating, "I don't appreciate pop cans left in the living room," than I do by saying, "The living room is a mess." I attract greater cooperation when my remarks are, "I don't enjoy getting out this mailing alone," than when I say, "You're all lazy and inconsiderate."

One reason people don't often respond favorably to evaluative criticism is that it is experienced as an attack. And attack is usually resisted and resented.

De-activate resistance and resentment by employing the *number one* rule of criticism. That rule is simply this — speak to the situation, not the person. Choose words that focus on what was accomplished or not accomplished, what exists or doesn't exist, what you feel or don't feel. Do not focus on the other person.

"*The report* was incomplete," speaks to the situation. "*You* did a lousy job," attacks the person.

"*It's* a quarter after 10:00," focuses on the situation. "Can't *you* remember to get here on time?" points to the person.

"I *missed three free throws* and fouled out," points to the situation. "*I played a terrible* game," puts the spotlight on me.

Listen to your criticism in the weeks ahead. Become increasingly aware of how you criticize yourself and others. When you hear yourself evaluating others or notice evaluative self-talk, STOP. Recall the number one rule of criticism — speak to the situation, not the person. Rephrase your criticisms. Share what you don't appreciate and describe what you see or hear. Then congratulate yourself for taking another step towards the language of acceptance and away from the judgment trap.

Summary

In this chapter you have read how language that judges, criticizes, and evaluates keeps you trapped in a state of non-acceptance. You have also learned about the destructive nature of words that compare, put-down and blame. You have been exposed to a style of language that can free you from the judgment trap and leave you in a place conducive to personal growth. You are now increasingly aware of the language of acceptance.

Beyond acceptance lies the language of confidence. In the chapter that follows, you will learn how to nurture yourself with self-talk that builds confidence and moves you to a new level of belief in yourself. Read on and experience the language of confidence.

Chapter Six

THE LANGUAGE OF CONFIDENCE

What is confidence? Where does it come from? Why do some people appear to overflow with confidence while others seem to be running on empty?

Confidence is a way of behaving that doesn't just happen. It occurs because people have learned to nurture themselves with self-talk that promotes confidence. It exists when individuals have learned to speak from faith rather than fear, from belief rather than doubt, from uniqueness rather than conformity.

Confident behaviors flow out of self-confident beliefs. And those beliefs are created by thinking self-confident thoughts using self-confident words.

Examine your self-talk right now. Is it full of doubt? Are you saying to yourself, "I'm afraid this chapter is going to be a washout," "If you can convince me, I'll give it a try," or "I sort of believe what you're saying"?

Or is your self-talk full of faith? Are you saying to yourself, "There is something here for me," "I'm going to enjoy this whether I agree with it or not," or "I expect this will be a juicy chapter"? Whatever your words concerning this chapter, remember that they will influence your behavior as you proceed through the pages that follow.

Hope

Are you hoping to find some useful strategies in this chapter to strengthen your level of confidence? Or are you hoping to find what you perceive as errors in my logic to diminish my credibility as a believable author? Either way, you are undermining your confidence by how you choose to program your mind. *Hope* is not part of the language of confidence. Instead, it signals doubt and low expectancy. It also promotes inertia.

You've heard the word used many times.

"I *hope* I get the raise."

"I sure *hope* they get here on time."

"I'm *hoping* for a set of golf clubs for my birthday."

"Now, what's wrong with hope?" you're probably wondering. "After all, isn't hope the one good thing Pandora found in the box after she turned loose all the evils of the world? Isn't hope our only salvation when everything else seems to be going wrong?"

Actually, hope promotes doubt. It helps your mind focus on uncertainty. If you *hope* you can learn to ride your new bike, you don't fully believe you can ride it. If you *hope* you passed the test, you're not certain. If you're *hoping* you'll get enough money together to take a vacation, you're expressing doubt about your ability to do it.

Hope is also a passive word. Like its cousin "wish," hope diminishes the chance that you'll take decisive action to do something about the undesired condition. When you hope or wish that things get better, when you hope or wish someone will come along to be your friend, when you hope or wish you had a new job, you're spending your present moments doing nothing about the conditions you hope or wish would change. By hoping or wishing, you inform your mind that you're already working on the problem. In that way, you prevent yourself from searching for solutions or taking any other direct action.

Hope is also unself-responsible. When you hope, you imply that something other than yourself, some external force is going to come to the rescue. You give up your own power when you hope. You rely on something "out there" to save you and provide that happy ending.

In spite of its drawbacks, my biggest concern with hope is that it's not strong enough. It is positive expectancy that attracts to us what we want in our lives, not hope. It is positive expectancy that sends messages of confidence to ourselves and others, not hope. Consider "if/when" programming.

If/When

"*If* I'm offered the new job, we'll take a two-week vacation."
"*When* I'm offered the new job, we'll take a two-week vacation."

"*If* I get a date, I'll buy that new shirt."
"*When* I get a date, I'll buy that new shirt."

"*If* I buy a new house, I want two bathrooms."
"*When* I buy a new house, I want two bathrooms."

What did you notice about the "if/when" statements? Which do you think sounds most powerful? Which do you believe gives you the best chance of getting what you want? Which one speaks to you of confidence and positive expectation?

I believe "if" breeds doubt and uncertainty. Its use is a signal that you lack confidence and also represents additional programming that undermines the confidence you do have. By using it, you decrease your chances of getting what you want now and in the future.

There's more faith in "when." Its use signifies positive expectancy and certainty. It is a clue that you feel confident in this area and at the same time strengthens your confidence programming.

When you act with certainty, you have a better chance of achieving your objective than when you act with uncertainty. You're more likely to act with certainty when you speak and think with certainty. "When" is language that programs your mind to expect and also strengthens your belief that you will get what you want. It is part of the language of confidence.

Expectation

Don't wish or hope for things. Know. To know is to be certain. I don't hope to find a publisher for this manuscript this summer. I know I will have one. I don't wish people will buy this book. I know they will buy it. And *when* those events happen, I'll *know* part of it was due to my use of the language of confidence.

We don't get from life any more than we expect. And we don't get any less than we expect either. Check your life. Look around. What have you created for yourself? What you see will give you some idea of what you've been expecting.

What you expect is what you get. It's called the self-fulfilling prophecy. And it works like this:

When you expect your children to act out and cause trouble, they act out and cause trouble. When you expect your work to be boring and unrewarding, it becomes boring and unrewarding. When you expect to finish last in the racquetball league, you finish last in the racquetball league.

Likewise, when you expect a happy marriage, you create a happy marriage for yourself. When you expect to have an abundance of friends, you have an abundance of friends. When you expect to enjoy your vacation, you enjoy your vacation.

There is power in expectation because your perception and behavior change with your expectations. When you expect to enjoy your vacation, you notice situations and circumstances that can be interpreted as enjoyable. You dwell on those, immerse yourself in them and choose enjoyment. When events and situations occur that could be viewed as boring, you don't notice them or, if you do, you don't interpret them as boring. You create an enjoyable vacation for yourself and your reality matches your expectations.

Similarly, when you expect to be miserable on your vacation, you notice those situations that can be interpreted as miserable. You dwell on those and revel in being miserable. When events occur that could be viewed as enjoyable, you don't notice, or interpret them as boring. With this programming, you create a miserable vacation for yourself and once again your reality matches your expectations.

What you expect is what you look for. What you look for is what you see. What you see is what you get. And what you get is what you look for in the future.

I know a woman who expected to get a cold every winter. Her words more than hinted at her expectations. "Every winter I get a cold," she would say. Or, "I wonder when I'll catch my cold this year?" One February I heard her remark, "You know, winter is almost over and I haven't had my cold yet."

You know what happens to this woman? Each year she gets a cold. And she uses each cold to strengthen her expectation for the next year. In a sense, she speaks with the language of confidence. She is confident she will get a cold. And her programming helps her create her reality.

You might be thinking that her expectations come from having had so many colds in the past. I disagree. Even if she experienced a cold for ten consecutive winters, she doesn't have to expect one the next year. Expectation is not fixed. It's an internal process over which each person has control. Her expectations are her choice.

Not only did this woman expect she would get a cold, she also expected her six-year-old son to get colds, too. "My mom says I get a lot of colds just like her," he told me once. "Mostly, I only get them in the winter, though," he continued. This youngster had already internalized the expectation of his mother. Her expectation was now his. Just like his mother, each winter he expected and got a number of colds.

I don't get colds in the winter or at any other time. I expect to be healthy. I don't have time for a cold. Colds are inconvenient and get in my way. I've got too many things I want to do to spend time dealing with colds. So I don't expect them.

Because I don't expect colds, I don't look for them. I don't notice every little itch or sniffle that could be interpreted as the start of a cold. I don't notice drafts or times I've forgotten my jacket on a cool night. I don't say things to myself like, "That sure was drafty. I'll probably get a cold." I don't have cold signals in my consciousness because I haven't programmed myself with language to help me expect colds.

Actually, I did get a cold this year. And because I didn't expect it, I was surprised. For three days I didn't believe it was a cold. Because I didn't believe it was a cold I acted as if I didn't have one. I ran fourteen miles one day with it and felt fine. I stayed on my work and exercise schedule. I didn't miss a step.

On the fourth day, I admitted to myself I had a cold. I continued to act and talk to myself as if I were surprised. "Wow, this sure is strange. I certainly don't get many colds. This cold helps remind me how few colds I get. It sure is nice to be a person who seldom gets colds." I continued to use language that supported my confidence in being a person who doesn't get colds. Because of how I choose to program my mind, I don't expect to get another one.

Just because you expect something is no guarantee that you will get it. And just because you expect not to get something else is no guarantee that you won't. However, expectation, both positive and negative, increases your chances. It ups the odds.

Positive expectation and the words that promote it gets the force of belief working for you. It puts the power of confidence on your side, working with you to achieve your goals.

Notice the confidence inherent in the following statements:

"I know this is going to be a great day."

"I expect a big turnout for the sale."

"I believe this report is a winner."

"I'm expecting to do well today."

Although there are no guarantees, language that connotes positive expectations gives you a better chance of getting what you want than language that speaks of negative expectations. Examine the sentences which follow to determine their direction and strength of expectation.

"I doubt if this day will be as good as yesterday."

"I wonder if this report is good enough?"

"I'm not expecting much from him."

"I believe we're going downhill."

You can believe you'll do well or poorly. You can expect a huge crowd or a small one. You can doubt your ability or have faith in it. The direction your belief and expectation takes is up to you. You control it. Why not let it work for you, moving you in a positive direction rather than a negative one?

Language of Confidence
Following a Demonstration

Since the language of confidence helps bring about desired events, it is important to use words of positive expectancy prior to the materialization of those desires. And it is just as important to implement the language of confidence immediately following their materialization. The next two incidents will help me describe that point.

I am a long distance runner, currently training to run my first marathon. I have run distances up to 15½ miles without stopping. I am currently on a schedule that calls for one long run of 14 miles or more each week.

On days when I do my long run, I drink a lot of water before I begin. When the temperature is in the 80's or 90's, my body can dehydrate quickly, so I store up before I start. It is also important to replenish some of the water I use up when I am out on the road. Therefore, I drink whenever I find water along my route.

I have a friend who also runs long distances. Before he begins his long run, he drives the route and leaves jars of water at appropriate places so he can drink it when he gets there. Or he plans his run to circle by a drinking fountain three or four times.

I don't plan water into my long runs because I *know* I will find it when I get out on the roads. I expect it. I know that someone will be washing his car, sprinkling her lawn or in some other way be waiting to offer me a drink. Therefore, I think thoughts that reinforce that knowing.

Because I expect to find water, I find it. I notice it, I hear it and I smell it. It doesn't always happen consciously, yet I've been able to find water in one way or another on all my runs.

I have splashed water on my face from a child's swimming pool, chatted with a man about growing vegetables while I interrupted the watering of his garden and admired a young woman in a bikini while I drank from the hose she was using to rinse her car. I've run through sprinklers and have requested that people spray me with hoses. The most unusual way I was presented with water occurred the day I became the welcome target of a water balloon.

The water-filled balloon arrived right on schedule one hot afternoon. I had run five miles without noticing any cars being washed or lawns being watered. Still I knew I would find water and expected it soon. At six miles, I was extremely thirsty and still hadn't produced any water. My faith continued. Around seven miles I saw a young boy step from his front door a block ahead of me. Intuitively, I knew something was going to happen, and that his coming out of the house at this time was connected to me in some way.

I was running on the opposite side of the street from his house. I watched as he walked across the lawn holding something behind his back. As I jogged to within his throwing distance, he launched the balloon in my direction and ran. It bounced once in front of me, hit the curb on the second bounce and flipped up into the air. I caught it as I ran rhythmically along never breaking stride.

My first impulse as I looked at this water balloon I was holding was to be surprised. My second was to laugh. "Of course," I thought to myself, "it's about time. I've been expecting some water." By saying to myself, "Of course, I've been expecting some water," I activated the language of confidence. I talked to myself as if I had expected the water, which indeed I had. And by doing so, I strengthened that expectation for the future.

Surprise Talk

I chose purposefully not to use surprise talk. I didn't say, "I don't believe this. This is incredible." I didn't talk as if I was surprised because I don't want to believe that receiving water on my runs from any source is incredible. I want to believe that it is natural and on time. Therefore, I chose language congruent with my expectation.

Running also provided me with another experience that helped me learn the importance of surprise talk.

I run 10,000 meter road races on the weekends. My time is usually around 43 minutes for that distance. Last year I began to lower that time with each race. Once I ran a 42:51, then a 42:15. The day I ran my fastest 10,000 meters ever at 41:37, I was elated. When my wife approached me to offer congratulations, I told her my time and said, "This is amazing!" She heard my words before I did. "Why would you choose to be amazed?" she asked.

Yes, I did elect to be a bit surprised at my time of 41:37. And that's not a situation where I want to be surprised or convey surprise to my subconscious mind. Given a choice, I want to choose language that reinforces my expectation of recording that time again. I want to choose words that promote confidence and certainty in order to develop beliefs about myself as a person who runs 41-minute 10,000 meter races. "I knew I could do it," I quickly said. "Of course I can run that fast. In fact, I'm surprised I didn't do it sooner!"

I recently heard a woman win a color television set on a radio call-in program. "I don't believe this is happening to me," were the first words out of her mouth. "Oh, I can't believe it," followed right behind. "Why not?" I wanted to ask her. "Don't you expect nice things to happen to you?"

Be careful about how you react to your own successes. Words like "Incredible," "Unbelievable" and "Amazing" are ways of programming your mind to expect less of the same in the future. Eliminate surprise talk from your repertoire. Remind yourself to expect the best. You deserve it.

Warnings

Your confidence programming and developing levels of expectation begin at birth. Your well-intentioned parents contributed to that programming through the use of loving warnings:

"Be careful, you'll fall."

"Watch out or you'll spill your milk."

"That could break if you're not careful."

"Keep an eye out for cars."

"Sit up close or you'll spill your food."

Warnings plant doubt in your mind. As significant others consistently doubt your abilities, you eventually begin to doubt them yourself. Imagine the effect of hearing many repetitions of "Be careful or you'll fall." Having been exposed to several variations on that theme, what kind of thoughts do you think you'd activate when you start to climb a tree or experiment with a stepladder? What kind of beliefs would you develop about yourself in relationship to heights? Would your behavior reflect a high degree of confidence?

"Sit up close or you'll spill your food," only needs to be repeated so many times before you begin to believe that if you don't sit up close, you'll spill food. "Watch out or you'll drop it," doesn't need to be voiced too many times before you begin to see yourself as a person who is liable to drop things.

Once you begin to believe you're liable to drop things or likely to spill food, it's just a matter of time before you act out the behaviors consistent with your programming. Since you believe you are a person who drops things, you act like a person who drops things. You don't act confident. You act nervous and doubt your abilities. Your actions become awkward and unsure. Naturally, because you are acting awkward and unsure, you are more likely to drop things. When you do drop something, you accumulate more evidence that you are indeed a person who drops things, and you continue to add to your programming. Eventually, you drop enough things to prove your belief to yourself.

Expectation in Disguise

Warnings we receive from others are disguised expectations. We are warned about spilling our milk by people who expect us to spill milk. We are warned about breaking things by people who expect us to break things. After repeated warnings, we begin to develop expectations of ourselves in line with the expectations of others. In time, we learn to expect to spill our food, fall or drop things. In this way, our insecurity programming is reinforced and grows stronger.

Evaluations

In addition to warnings, we have also been programmed in our early years by the evaluations of others. If your parents consistently evaluated your memory as poor, you may have begun to expect your memory to be poor. If your teachers continually pointed out what a troublemaker you were, you may have come to think of yourself as a troublemaker. If your father frequently called you a loser, you can imagine what view of yourself could have developed.

Playmates and classmates added to your programming. Put-downs, name calling and labeling as described in Chapter Five were the tools they used. Each helped you create a picture of yourself as clumsy, fat, shy or unworthy.

If you heard how fat you were enough times, you may have begun to talk to yourself as if you were fat. If friends were constantly talking about your shyness, you may have internalized a picture of yourself as shy. If your clumsiness was pointed out repeatedly, you may have come to believe you are a clumsy person.

Self-Responsibility

As young children, we are particularly susceptible to the programming that originates in others, especially from people who are important to us. Even though significant others supplied much of our early programming, it would be a mistake to blame who we are today on the programming we received from them as children. That view is not self-responsible and ignores the choice we now have in the process.

Just because someone calls you fat, doesn't mean you have to accept it. Whether or not someone calls you fat is their choice. Whether or not you internalize it and begin to call yourself fat is your choice. In the end it matters less what programming you receive and matters more what programming you believe.

It is what you tell yourself about what others tell you that counts the most. If someone judges you as stupid and you buy in to that interpretation, it is more your agreement with the interpretation that programs your mind than the judgment itself. If, on the other hand, you don't accept their judgment, it is your disagreement with it that creates your mindset. Either way, you control your own programming. Regardless of what others attempt to lay on you, you are responsible.

Occasionally, people like to argue for their limitations here. "My parents made me feel like a loser when I was very young," a woman once told me. "I was too young to know better. It's their fault I have low self-esteem and no confidence. How can you say I had a choice? I wasn't old enough or strong enough to emotionally resist their programming."

Certainly young children are more easily influenced by the significant people in their lives than are mature adults. Still, the ultimate responsibility for what you choose to feel or internalize based on the programming you received as a child rests with you. Look at it this way.

Let's assume that as a child you were subjected to countless judgments and put-downs. Let's also say you were continually criticized for your efforts and no matter what you did it was never good enough. Praise was something that didn't exist in your childhood. Your parents withheld love when your behavior didn't match their expectations, which was most of the time. Let's assume also that they fought a lot, got a divorce and blamed it on you.

As a result of being exposed to this environment, you developed low confidence, poor self-esteem and a drinking problem. Now you want to believe that your drinking problem, your low self-esteem and your lack of confidence is the fault of your parents? Before you argue further for the validity of that belief, consider the following.

Look closely at the children from large families, especially families where the home environment is not pleasant. Some of those children turn out bitter, resentful and act out lives of revenge and resistance. Others develop a more positive outlook and seemingly reject their early programming. This phenomenon occurs with children from the same family who receive almost identical experiences in a similar environment.

What is the difference? It's not in the parents, the life experiences or the environment. The difference lies within each individual child. It is the interpretations each child attaches to the circumstances and situations in his life. It is in the words he says to himself about what is going on around him. The difference lies in his self-talk.

Some people take their parents' negative programming to heart, agree with it, and conform to it. Others deny it internally and then withdraw or act out in defiance. Some people play deaf and let the negative messages pass right through without giving them a second thought. Others struggle to overcome the programming and become positive, happy and easy to get along with. There are as many different reactions to the programming as there are people who react to it.

Your parents may well have treated you poorly. In fact, you might have had the worst parents in the world. In spite of what your parents were, or how they treated you, they are not responsible for your reactions to them. You are.

Even if your parents were responsible for the early programming that made you what you are today, they aren't responsible any longer. Those days are over. If you are full of programming that contains low self-esteem and lack of confidence messages, it is because you continue to perpetuate those messages with self-talk that supports and strengthens them.

You're older now and more mature. If, at the time, you weren't able to reject the negative programming you received as a child, you can do it now. There's no useful reason to continue to give power to the messages that were inaccurate years ago and continue to be invalid today. You can take charge of your own programming and change it. One way to do that is through the use of affirmations.

Affirmations

Use of affirmations is a strategy designed to put you in charge of your own programming. It is a method for learning to talk to yourself in self-enhancing ways that will reprogram your mind with positive messages about yourself.

An affirmation is a positive thought you intentionally choose to place in your mind to achieve a result you desire. Some examples follow:

- I am lovable and capable.
- I am happy and friendly around other people.
- I am a positive person.
- I have the wisdom necessary to handle conflicts in loving ways.
- I am peaceful and calm.
- I have everything necessary to enjoy this moment.
- I am accepting and loving of other people.
- My memory is strong and accurate.
- I speak self-responsible words. I think self-responsible thoughts.

The use of affirmations is a way to reprogram your mind through repetitious thought. It is a way of taking control and re-minding yourself with the words, phrases and sentences that you want in your bio-computer.

I don't remember where or when I first heard about affirmations. I do recall the first one I ever used and the result it produced. The results were timely and helpful, and I have been fine tuning this technique for use in my life ever since.

"I, Chick Moorman, am a positive person," was my first affirmation. I designed it for myself because I was sick of being negative. At that point in my life I was unhappy, hostile and continually looking to find fault. I was telling myself that I was right and everyone else was wrong. My self-talk was negative, my thinking was negative and the results I generated were negative. Daily, I proved to myself how awful my world was and my only solace came from brief moments of basking in the glory that I was right.

"I, Chick Moorman, am a positive person," became the first of a steady flow of affirmations I designed to re-mind myself and create a reality consistent with how I wanted to live my life. I began by writing my first affirmation ten times each morning. I also repeated it to myself for a few minutes while I jogged.

Almost immediately I noticed a change in my life. The day after I started using the reprogramming phrase, a woman approached me in the grocery store and commented on my attractive shirt. I thought to myself, "Surely this woman can see how positive I am. Otherwise she never would have approached me." Only one day and my affirmation was working. I wrote it the next day with increased confidence and belief.

The following day, while I was out running, a young child spotted me. As he ran along in front of his home, he shouted, "Hey, mister. See me? I'm a runner, too." "Wow! Now even little kids can sense how positive I am," I thought to myself. "This affirmation stuff is really powerful."

As the weeks passed, I continued to say and write my affirmation. I also continued to stockpile evidence that I was indeed a positive person. People increased their friendliness towards me. (Or was I increasing my friendliness towards them?) More positive things started happening in my life. (Or was I simply noticing the positive more often?) It didn't matter. I didn't care which came first. I was content just to have it happen.

The more evidence I received that I was a positive person, the more I began to act like a positive person. The more I acted positively, the more I noticed that I was positive. And the cycle continued.

People started reacting to me in new ways. My old negative friends stopped coming around. It wasn't fun for them to complain and criticize around me when I was being positive. New friends started appearing in my life. I began to attract people who thought the way I was now thinking.

Because I was thinking positively and acting positively, my life events seemed more positive. Was it simply that I was seeing these events in a more positive light or were these events really more positive? Probably some of both. It didn't matter. The end result was that my life was more positive and that was the way I wanted it.

Armed with this powerful new technique, I set out to change other areas of my life as well. My weight and my writing were two areas I wanted to effect immediately so I designed an affirmation for each.

"I, Chick Moorman, am a streamlined person. I think streamlined thoughts. I make streamlined choices." That became my weight affirmation. I reprogrammed myself with these sentences over a period of one year. In that time, I lost 30 pounds, went from a size 38 waist to a size 32 and tightened the muscles throughout my body. Today, I weigh in at a streamlined 160 pounds and like it.

"I, Chick Moorman, am an author. I write a book which uplifts, illuminates and helps people find direction in their lives." I designed this affirmation because I was struggling to develop consistency in my writing. My first book, *Our Classroom: We Can Learn Together,* which I wrote with my wife, Dee, took five years to complete. The first four years were a series of starting and stopping, believing and giving up, and writing in spurts. It seemed as though we would never become published authors.

Immediately following the use of my new affirmation, we signed a contract with Prentice-Hall for *Our Classroom.* With the help of the reprogramming phrases that reminded me that I was an author, we finished the book in one year. As you read this, I am the published author of two books, and have others in mind. I have no doubt that my use of affirmations, which helped me believe in myself as an author and focused my mind in that direction, is one of the major reasons why my name appears in card catalogues today.

Why Affirmations Work

There are several theories as to why affirmations work. The religious theory holds that affirmations are like prayer. God hears the prayer (affirmation) and responds.

A psychologist might suggest that affirmations are related to the subconscious mind. In that theory, it is believed that affirmations plant ideas in the subconscious mind and when this part of your mind senses an appropriate situation, it sends your conscious mind a signal. You then act in accordance with what you have been affirming.

A third theory is that thoughts have energy. The energy from an affirmation goes out into the world, has an impact on people and objects, and attracts situations and circumstances that contain similar energy patterns.

I'm not sure which of those theories is correct, if any. And I don't care. I only care that they work and that I know how to use the process. It's like my microwave oven. I have no idea why it works. I put food in, set the dial, push a button, and the food comes out hot and juicy.

It doesn't matter to me whether affirmations are a prayer, have energy or stimulate the subconscious mind. All I care is that I know how to pop them in, set the dial, push the button, and have the important issues of my life come out hot and juicy.

Although I don't know exactly how affirmations work, I do have some insights into the process. Here is my sense of how it all happens.

Affirmations help me put thoughts into my mind of what I want. Repetitious thought reprograms my mind and adds strength to my wants. The more often I have these thoughts, the more I expect them. The stronger my expectations become, the more I pay attention to and notice them when they occur. The more I notice them, the stronger my expectation becomes and the more I believe they will happen in the future. And this cycle continues to repeat itself, growing stronger with every revolution.

Design Your Own Affirmations

Spend time now designing affirmations for yourself. What is it you want to create for yourself in your life? What are your wants? Do you want happiness, confidence, money, weight loss or more friends? Any characteristic, object, personality trait, attitude or circumstance can be affirmed into existence. Think about what it is that *you* want.

On a piece of paper write down fifteen things you want in your life. These could include a new lover, health, improved golf scores, joy, a positive outlook, completion of a project, honesty, recognition, or a new house. Write your fifteen now.

Examine your list closely and determine which three are the most significant to you. Which three are so important that you'd be willing to spend some time each day attracting them into your life? Which three are so important that you'd be willing to spend time and energy designing an affirmation for yourself?

Take the time now, before you read on, to write an affirmation for your three most important wants. Design them so they fit you.

Start by writing your affirmations as if the condition you want already exists. "I am a positive person," is a stronger affirmation than "I am capable of being a positive person." "I am confident," is more useful than "I will be confident."

If you really don't believe you are confident or positive right now, your mind may not accept that affirmation. Begin instead with, "I am becoming increasingly confident" or "I grow more positive every day." When you've gathered some evidence and you start to prove your confidence to yourself, then you can switch over to the stronger, "I am a confident person."

Tips on Affirmations

1. *Be Selective:* Ten affirmations are a lot to concentrate on at one time. I suggest you start with one. After you experience positive effects and strengthen your belief in this tool, you can use two or three at a time.

2. *Variety:* Say your affirmations aloud. Repeat them silently to yourself. Record them on tape and play them back to yourself. Write them. Sing them. Repeat them in monotone.

3. *Consistency:* Say or write your affirmations regularly. Create the habit of doing it at the same time each day. You can do them first thing in the morning, before you go to bed, at 10 a.m. each day or over the lunch hour. Using affirmations will give you the opportunity to practice self-discipline. Use that opportunity. Not only will you be helped by your affirmations, you will also learn to see yourself as a self-disciplined person.

4. *Following a Demonstration:* A useful time to say or write affirmations is immediately following a demonstration of your expectation. If you have been writing, "I am a runner," and you just completed your first 5K race, then that's an important time to say your affirmation to yourself. If your affirmation has been "I live in abundance," and you get a $25

check in the mail, use that occasion to repeat your affirmation a few times. Your belief is strongest following a demonstration that confirms it. That's when your affirmation will carry the most power. Use that time to further strengthen your belief.

5. *Appreciate:* As you begin to use affirmations, you will notice small signs of success. Be appreciative and know that more is coming. If you are affirming wealth and find a dollar, you have two choices. You can say, "Gee, only a dollar. I guess it's not working." Or you can think, "Wow! A dollar. I'm on my way now!" See the dollar as evidence that more abundance is on the way. Congratulate yourself for your success. Appreciate the flow that you have already begun.

6. *Persist:* Your current beliefs, expectations and attitudes are the result of years of programming. It doesn't seem likely that you will change all that by writing affirmations two days in a row. It takes time. Be patient and continue your mental work. You will reprogram your mind if you stick with it.

7. *Positive Picturing:* In addition to programming your mind with words, you can also use images or visualizations. You can strengthen your affirmation by adding a positive image to it.

If your affirmation is, "I am a streamlined person," create a symbolic visual image of yourself as streamlined. See yourself as if the condition you desire already exists. Put a picture in your mind of yourself as streamlined.

Immediately following the writing of your affirmations, use the next two or three minutes to do positive picturing. Relax. Think of your affirmation. Place the positive picture in your mind. See yourself standing in front of the mirror at the desired weight. Or see yourself trying on new clothes, two sizes smaller than you are now. Hold on to that image for a few minutes. Enjoy it. Then let it go, forget about it and go on with your daily activities.

The visualizations I used with my affirmation on being an author were extremely vivid. I used two. One was of me autographing books in bookstores, at conferences and workshops. The other was seeing this book in bookstores on the rack that lists the top twenty best sellers. I watched it go from thirteenth to ninth to third to number one.

8. *Emotionality:* Put some strong feeling with your affirmations. When you are picturing or affirming, create the feel-

ings of what it would be like to actually have that condition exist in your life. Feel happy, joyous, ecstatic. Smile. Experience on an emotional level how much you will enjoy the manifestation of your affirmation.

Bumper Stickers

Bumper stickers, sometimes referred to as auto-suggestions, are another way to program your mind to produce what you want. These phrases are similar to affirmations, differing in one respect. They are shorter. Examples include:

> Go for it.
> Take a full cut.
> My point of power is *Now*.
> Act as if.
> To give is to receive.
> I don't settle.
> I make no exceptions.
> Do it now.
> I deserve it.
> Now is all there is.
> Being right doesn't work.
> I'm enough.
> Be the one.

These quick phrases can help you develop more confidence and a greater sense of personal power in your life. Pick one that holds strong meaning for you. Write it 20 times, once a day for one week. This repetitious writing will plant the phrase in your mind. Later, when you can use it, the phrase will flash into your awareness.

When your mind returns the bumper sticker to you, it is a signal to act. Put it to use immediately. If you have been writing, "Do it now," and your mind sends you that message, don't hesitate. Do it now.

Don't settle, take a full cut, act as if or go for it. Whatever you have been working on, follow through when you get the signal. The more often you respond to the message, the more often your mind will send it when you want it. If you ignore the message and don't act, your mind will stop sending it. If you abuse it, you lose it.

Affirmation and bumper stickers are ways to take back the responsibility for programming your mind from radio, T.V., your parents, teachers and friends. Remember, if you don't program your own mind, someone else will. What better person to have in charge of the programming that enters your bio-computer than you, yourself?

Affirming

Affirmation and bumper stickers are strategies to use at specific times to create or attract specific characteristics, abilities or situations into your life. While it is important and useful to use these structured processes to achieve specific results, it is of equal value to develop an ongoing style of talking to yourself that is affirmative and self-supportive. Learning to continually affirm yourself is a way of giving yourself supportive programming that can become more than a tool. It can become a way of life.

During a recent conversation, a friend explained to me how disgusted she was with herself for not sharing her anger with a person she felt had taken advantage of her. A year ago this friend of mine wasn't skilled at recognizing her own feelings, much less expressing them. She had grown tremendously in that year. Through a lot of work and effort on her part, she is now able to notice her feelings and name them accurately.

On the day I talked with her, she had created depression by getting after herself with self-talk that berated her failure to communicate her negative feelings. "I'm not very gutsy if I can't tell her I'm angry," "What a scaredy cat I am," and "I'm no good if I'm afraid," were examples of her internal dialogue. She not only wasn't nurturing herself, she was beating herself up with self-talk.

Far healthier for my friend to choose nourishing words and concentrate on the growth she had made. "I sure am getting quick at recognizing my feelings," "I certainly am noticing my feelings better than I have in the past," and "I'm getting closer to the way I want to be," are examples of supportive self-talk she could have used.

Supportive self-talk is dialogue that recognizes your successes and gives yourself credit for them. It leaves you in a healthier place from which to contemplate change. That doesn't mean you don't recognize some things you'd like to change or are totally happy with everything you do. It only means you concentrate on your successes and give yourself some credit.

You can parent yourself with words that nourish or words that judge and criticize. You can speak to yourself with language that reveals self-respect or self-condemnation. You can use words that strengthen your belief in yourself or those that raise suspicion concerning your abilities. In short, you can affirm yourself or use language that denies your strengths and worth.

Language of Denial

My friend who spoke to herself with "I'm no good," and "I'm not very gutsy," was using the language of denial. Denial is a style of language that puts down or diminishes your capabilities, choices, power, talents and accomplishments. It works in opposition to both the language of confidence and the language of acceptance.

The language of denial can be as simple as labeling yourself with judgmental names such as stupid, lazy, frigid or boring, as described in Chapter Five. Or it can be as complicated as a lengthy apology preceding a presentation or an extended excuse rationalizing your behavior.

Speaking of yourself as limited, incomplete or unskilled is one category of the language of denial.

"That's over my head."
"It's too deep for me."
"I'll never figure it out."
"I'll be sunk for sure."

Self-talk like the sentences above deny your capability and focus on your limitations. They put down your abilities and talents, and build a belief that you are not enough. When you speak to yourself this way, your words perpetuate behaviors that are consistent with that view. Because you behave in accordance with your belief, you eventually prove it to yourself. The next step is to follow the proof of your not enoughness with even more negative self-talk that highlights your perceived limits and incompleteness.

Instead of talking to yourself as if you're not enough, you can choose words that affirm your limitlessness and completeness. You can speak to yourself with the language of confidence.

"That's right up my alley."

"I can handle that."

"I'll figure that out for sure."

"This is a piece of cake for me."

Perhaps, though, you hold deep seated beliefs that you are limited and incomplete. In that case, it would be of little value to try to talk yourself into something that is totally opposed to those beliefs. If you are firmly convinced that something will be difficult for you, don't attempt to forcefully convince yourself. Instead, shift your focus. Concentrate on some other aspect of the same situation that is easier to accept. Mention your persistence or your tenacity. Choose phrases that help you see yourself as worthy. Find something you can believe in and talk to yourself about that.

Instead of, "It's too deep for me," say "That's pretty deep so I'll stick with it until I get it." Replace "I'll never figure it out," with "It may take awhile, and with my persistence I'll figure it out." "I may have to struggle, so I'll stay on top of this one," can be used instead of "I'll be sunk for sure."

Speaking to yourself in doubting language is another way to implement the language of denial.

"I'm not sure I can do this."

"I really haven't received any training in this area."

"I don't know about me."

The sentences above contain language that reveal distrust in yourself. They are a signal that you lack confidence.

In addition to announcing a lack of confidence, the language choices above also undermine the confidence you do have. They become programming that chips away at your existing confidence and promotes doubt, which adds to your vulnerability.

Reject phrases that proclaim doubt. If you are unsure about yourself in a situation, acknowledge that the experience is new or unique for you. Then add words of confidence about your ability to handle new experiences.

"I really haven't received any training in this area," is language that denies your capableness. It helps you focus on a limitation, your lack of training.

"I've not received training in this area and I learn fast," accentuates your capableness. It helps you focus on a strength, your ability to learn fast.

Choose programming that puts the focus where it does the most good. Use language that speaks to your strengths. Talk sense to yourself.

Winning and Losing

Develop the habit of talking to yourself as a winner. When you stop comparing yourself to others and focus on your strengths, this becomes easier to do. Use self-praise, affirmations and thoughts about your capabilities. Speak positively of your success, your achievements and your effort.

Never speak of yourself as a loser. If you fail at something, that doesn't mean you're a failure. That doesn't mean you won't succeed at it next week or even tomorrow. It only means you're not doing it right now.

I recently observed a young man in a shopping center proudly displaying a patch on his blue jeans. "Born to Lose" was the message he chose to wear. I cringed as I read the words, knowing the impression that phrase was making on this man's consciousness.

Why would anyone want to believe he was born to lose, I wondered? Why would this young person prominently display such a negative expectation? And why would anyone purposefully sell such negative self-fulfilling messages?

Not everyone knows the relationship between language and belief, I concluded. Not everyone realizes the self-fulfilling nature of words and phrases. Not everyone understands how we program ourselves for winning and losing.

You do. You know now that the self-talk you engage in throughout the day programs you for self-doubt or for self-confidence. You know that it helps you to see yourself as able or unable, responsible or irresponsible, powerful or powerless.

You also realize by now that you have the potential to speak to yourself in any way you choose. You can speak to yourself as if you are weak or strong, clumsy or athletic, ugly or attractive, shy or confident. Since how you talk to yourself helps form your beliefs, and since you prove your beliefs to yourself, why not choose to talk to yourself as if you are able, responsible, powerful, strong, athletic, attractive, confident and whole? Your words are self-fulfilling. Why not choose words that get you what you want? Why not wear a patch on your jeans that announces, "Born to Win"?

Apologizing

Apologizing for yourself before beginning an activity is another form of the language of denial. Perhaps you've heard yourself using examples similar to these:

"Before I begin, I want to apologize for my voice. I have a cold today."

"I don't know what you'll think of this, but . . ."

"I'm sorry if this doesn't turn out well. It's the first time I've tried this recipe."

"My office is such a mess. I just haven't had a chance to clean it up."

Apologizing for yourself preceding an event is a sign of low self-esteem and lack of confidence. It is a signal to yourself and others that you are unsure. It's a way of denying your own worth and ability.

Apologizing ahead of time does not mean, "I'm sorry." It really means if I mention this situation first, then you won't be able to. In that sense, it's a manipulative attempt to control another person's behavior.

Apologizing is taking an "I'm just a nobody" stance. It communicates a willingness to take blame before anyone sends any. It puts you down and the other person up, and leaves you with a lower sense of personal power. It subtracts from an already shaky base of confidence.

When you notice yourself in the act of apologizing, stop. Ask yourself if you are really sorry. If not, skip the apology and the negative denial that goes with it.

Apologizing even after the fact is not necessary. If you are truly sorry for something you did, just tell the person involved what you've learned and that you're going to work at not doing it again. That's enough. You don't have to do remorse and regret to learn from your mistakes. And learning from mistakes is what's really important anyway, not beating yourself up with negative words and feelings.

"I learned you don't like me eating all the leftover pie without asking if you want any, and it's my intention not to do that again," leaves you feeling more powerful and self-responsible than, "I'm sorry I ate all the pie and I apologize. Please forgive me."

"I relearned how important it is to you that I call when I'm going to be late," leaves you with more esteem and self-confidence than, "I apologize for not calling you. I don't know what I was thinking about. I'm sorry."

The apologetic "I'm sorry" dance leaves you focusing on your mistakes, feeling small, and hoping to be forgiven. It is communication that lowers your self-esteem, personal power and confidence. The non-apologetic "I learned and I intend" position helps you focus on your learning and future intention. It implies no desire to be forgiven, nor reason to forgive. It is communication that keeps your self-esteem intact while enhancing your sense of personal power and confidence.

Exaggeration

Exaggeration is another more subtle version of the language of denial. Exaggeration communicates that you or your thoughts and ideas are not enough. In order to have importance, your ideas must be surrounded by inflated figures, statements or opinions. When you add exaggeration, you deny your ability to stand on what is. It's another way of telling yourself you are not enough.

It's not necessary to add 50 feet to the home run, 6 inches to the size of the fish or 30° to the temperature the day you walked across the desert alone without shoes. You're O.K. even if the home run was a single, the fish was undersized and the desert was a sand dune in November. You are enough just the way you are.

Bragging

Bragging, another variation of the language of denial, is related to exaggeration. Each is a clue that your esteem and confidence is low. Both spin out of a desire to be enough and a belief that you aren't. Bragging is an attempt to communicate, "Look how wonderful I am." Paradoxically, the message you send yourself when you boast to others is, "I'm not wonderful, so I had better cover that with a barrage of words."

Bragging is not to be confused with sharing positive information about yourself. Talking about your capabilities with others without exaggeration in a precise, soft-spoken manner is not bragging. It is simply sharing information, which is often useful to both you and the other party.

In workshops I frequently have participants practice giving information without boasting by milling around the room greeting each other and sharing a positive message about themselves with each person they greet.

"I want you to know," says person A, "I'm good at photography." "Thank you for sharing that," responds person B and "I want you to know I listen well."

After fifteen or twenty similar exchanges, a group discussion follows. Participants frequently report they didn't like announcing the positive message to others. "It feels like bragging," they say. I'm usually surprised at the number of participants who feel uncomfortable saying nice things about themselves. It's as if they believe that affirming themselves publicly is egotistical. Far better to remain small, insignificant, and innocuous than to be judged as a braggart, they think.

Because people incorrectly interpret communicating positives as boastful, they refrain from saying nice things about themselves in the presence of others. When they do so, they implement another variation of the language of denial — silence. By saying nothing, they diminish themselves by downplaying their own strengths and abilities.

Following this exercise participants also report they like hearing about the strengths of others. They find it useful, they contend, to know what other people are good at. "I never would have known that if you hadn't shared it," is a typical remark. "I really think it's interesting that you do that well," is another.

Sharing strengths can be useful to others. How else will other people know you play a respectable game of racquetball, enjoy cooking or run 10,000 meters in under 40 minutes unless you tell them? How will you know others are the lead guitar player, an accomplished pianist or grower of orchids unless they tell you?

It's interesting to me that some participants interpret saying positives as bragging. Yet hearing positives from others doesn't sound like bragging to them at all. In fact, they appreciate receiving the information.

There is a fine line between bragging and giving information. Sharing information becomes bragging when it contains exaggeration or is done in a loud or boastful manner. Information shared with a desire to impress or manipulate others is also a form of bragging. When you are more concerned with giving the other person useful information than you are with raising your stock in their eyes, you are not bragging.

"I make a tasty pizza," is giving information. "I'm the best pizza-maker in the world," is bragging. "I ran fourteen miles today," is giving information. "I ran like crazy today. Fourteen miles. Two hours and six minutes. Only stopped once for water. I was incredible," is bragging.

Practice giving information to yourself this week. Begin today. Stand in front of the mirror and affirm yourself by saying some of your strengths aloud. "I enjoy the consistency with which I run," "I feel really good about my writing ability," and "I like the way I address large groups of people," are some that I say about me. What are yours? Resist the temptation to put them down or silently implement the language of denial. Say them aloud. Do it now and add to your growing programming with the language of confidence.

Other Variations of the Language of Denial

Jargon

Using legal language, educationese, computer talk, or governmental semantics is another way to implement the language of denial. When you use the jargon of any institution, agency or association, you deny your own language and yourself by falling back on the false sense of self-esteem you mistakenly believe comes from using jargon.

Titles

Titles like *Dr.* Jones, *Mister* McMaster, *Reverend* Frasky and *Coach* Hoskins are labels that help you focus on authority.

This type of labeling puts the other person above you and relegates you to an inferior position. It denies your status as an equal, creates separateness, and does nothing to enhance your confidence.

Drop titles from your vocabulary. Refuse to use them. Go beyond labeling and use people's first names. Dr. Jones is also Mary Ann Jones. Mister McMaster's name is Bill. Enjoy the intimacy that comes from addressing other people as equals by using first names.

Practice using people's names when you talk to them. Put names at the beginning of a sentence. "Jack, I like the way you did that." Or use names to end your sentence. "Nice shot, Virginia." And throw in some sentences that use the person's name in the middle. "I'd like to thank you, Robert, for your efforts on this committee."

Watch the reactions you get when you address people by their first names. And monitor your own reactions. See if you don't feel increased intimacy and a narrowing of separateness.

Conformity

When moving towards increasing your sense of personal power, it is tempting to borrow words from people whom you judge as powerful. Resist that temptation. Using language and speech mannerisms that imitate someone else belies your individuality and brands you as a conformist. When you imitate others, the image you project is not natural. Observers are quick to spot the pretense and you come across as a copy, rather than as the unique, special person that you are.

Develop your own style of communicating. When you speak as your genuine self, you trust that you are enough. That confidence comes across to others as well as to you. Be yourself. You are worth it.

Quotations

Consistently quoting others indicates you believe that it is necessary to supplement your words with theirs. The unspoken message you send yourself is that your words and you are not enough. When you quote others, you deny your ability to share your own opinion without help.

When you consistently refer to others' words, you tell yourself and others that what you quoted has more value because someone else said it. You deny the value of sending the message in your own words. By that denial, you tell yourself that your voice, your words, and you are not as valuable as the person quoted.

Quoting others places that person above you and ranks their thoughts and style of expression above yours. That helps you assume a "little me, big you" stance.

When you're tempted to quote an authority or expert, stop. Remember that you too are an expert, in fact, you are the most qualified person in the world to describe your beliefs and express your thoughts and opinions. Think over the quote you are about to share. Decide whether or not you believe it or feel strongly about it. If you do, put the concepts in your own words. Speak with the language of confidence, the confidence that you alone can best express what's real for you.

Asking Questions

Often the questions we ask are not questions at all. Rather they are statements about us that we lack the confidence to express.

As a workshop leader, I often hear unspoken statements from participants that are disguised as questions. "Don't you think running can hurt you?" really means, "I think running can hurt you." "Don't you think children need more discipline?" means, "I think children need more discipline." "Do you feel it's necessary to practice this language *all* the time?" really means, "I'm not sure it's necessary for me to practice this language so often."

Stop denying the importance of your opinions and feelings. Turn your questions into statements and enjoy the reactions of others as you use one more strategy in the language of confidence.

Watering Down

"I guess/sort of/kind of" phrases water down your statements and weaken your sense of personal power.

"*I guess* I'll go."

"It was *kind of* exciting to be there."

"Guess/sort of/kind of" are words of hesitancy. They don't communicate confidence, self-respect, or belief in yourself. They respresent a technique to hedge the bet and take less than full responsibility for your statements.

The next time you hear yourself say "sort of" or "kind of" or "I guess," stop. Repeat the sentence without the self-limiting phrase. Pay attention to how it sounds. If it stands alone, fine. If not, forget it altogether.

Verbal Qualifiers

Qualifying your statements erodes both their strength and your confidence.

"I have this *little* consulting business."

"This is *only* my opinion."

"I'm playing well *for a change*."

Why qualify your statement by telling someone (and yourself) you have a "little" business? Why not let the statement stand alone? "I have a consulting business," is enough. That statement is accurate and also carries the flavor of pride and confidence.

Listen to the difference as you say the following statements aloud.

"This is my opinion."

or

"This is only my opinion."

"I'm playing well."

or

"I'm playing well for a change."

Which programming do you want fed into your bio-computer? Which phrases do you choose to have strengthening your beliefs?

Prediction

Words of prediction can be used to strengthen or undermine your confidence. Examine the sentences starters which follow:

"I'll be miserable when . . ."

"I won't like it if . . ."

"That'll be embarrassing."

In each case above, the anticipated event has not yet occurred. Yet the speaker, through his choice of verbal programming, has already started the mental process that will help define his response.

If I say or think, "I'll be miserable when I'm transferred to Des Moines," then there is a greater chance I'll activate miser-

143

able feelings and do miserable behaviors when I'm transferred. If I say or think, "I won't like it if the meeting runs overtime," then I've increased my chances of feeling annoyed when the meeting goes beyond the stated time limit.

A clear example of how predictions manifest into reality happened to a fifth-grade teacher I worked with. One of her students misbehaved often. Her relationship with this child was strained and several times I overheard her describe it to other teachers this way — "He makes my blood boil. He's going to be the death of me yet."

Not surprisingly, two months later during a routine examination this teacher was informed she had extremely high blood pressure. She was advised to take time off and was granted a medical leave of absence for a month.

Why not make positive predictions? How about using words that help you create the type of responses to life's situations that are confident and esteem-enhancing?"

"I'll make it through this and come out stronger."

"Either way, I'll be able to handle this."

"Working through conflict will strengthen our relationship."

If you're going to make predictions, have them be predictions that program your bio-computer with confidence. Predict strength, ability, effort and able-ness. Predict success.

Empty Words

"Uh-huh's," "hmm's" and "you know's" are patterns of speech that communicate lack of confidence. They are empty words used to fill time and space.

"You know" is an attempt to gain agreement from the listener. When you use it you ask for approval and permission to go on.

"We rowed to the middle of the lake, you know? It happened on my first cast, you know? The fish hit with such force, you know, it almost pulled me out of the boat, you know?"

To speak with confidence, it isn't necessary to get agreement or permission to continue. Think about what you have to say. If it isn't worthwhile, forget it. If it is, say it deliberately without the addition of empty words. Eliminate "uh-huh's," "hmm's" and "you know's" and add to your sense of personal power.

Indecision destroys confidence and weakens self-esteem. Consider the following:

"Maybe we can go tomorrow."

"Let me think about it for awhile."

"I'm not sure about that."

Do these statements sound to you like they come from a confident person? Consistent use of this style of language communicates indecision, procrastination and a denial of personal responsibility.

The language of confidence contains juicy yes's and juicy no's. It has no room for maybe's.

Learning to say *no* without guilt or shame is required for speaking confidently. Adding excuses, explanations and reasons for turning down a request are not necessary. You have a right to say *no* and it's O.K. if that *no* stands alone.

Fuzzy no's work against the language of confidence. A fuzzy no occurs when the person asking doesn't know whether or not you said no. I asked a friend if he wanted to have dinner with me next Thursday and he answered, "I'm scheduled to attend a PTA meeting next Thursday." Now, what does that mean? Where do I stand with this person? Did he want to have dinner with me or not? Because his no was fuzzy, I wasn't sure if he'd like to have dinner some other time or if he just wanted me to forget it. I would have preferred him to say,

> "I'd love to have dinner with you. I'm already committed to a PTA meeting that night. How about Wednesday?"

or

"No, I'd prefer not to."

or simply

"No, thank you."

Since I prefer juicy *yes's* or juicy *no's*, I hung right in there. When my friend responded, "I'm scheduled to attend a PTA meeting next Thursday night," I informed him he hadn't answered my question. "What do you mean?" he asked. I went on to explain that I hadn't asked whether he *would or could* have dinner with me Thursday night. I asked did he want to have dinner with me next Thursday. By hanging in there and demanding a juicy *yes* or juicy *no*, I got what I wanted. He said, "No."

"*No*," I can deal with. "Maybe," "I'll think about it," and fuzzy no's are more difficult to handle. They are open to so many different interpretations.

Some people hesitate to say *no* because they incorrectly believe they'll hurt another person's feelings. The clearer you become in your own mind that people can only hurt their own feelings, the easier it will become for you to say no. The more comfortable you get with surrendering to the reality that others are in charge of their feelings, the less you will try to control their emotional responses. As you become increasingly in tune with that belief, you will more often make decisions based on whether or not you really want to and less on how the other person might choose to feel.

You're doing no one a favor when you say *yes* and mean *no*. You're not being kind to yourself because you've now committed yourself to something you don't want to do. When you follow through, chances are you'll lack enthusiasm, feel like a martyr or be resentful. You'll then act in subtle ways that communicate your resentment.

You're not being kind to the other person either. You've now deprived her of the kindest message you could offer, the truth. At the same time, you've prevented her from finding someone else who would enjoy her company. All this because you didn't want to hurt her feelings by saying *no*.

The more comfortable you become with hearing *no* from others, the easier it will become for you to use the word yourself. Once you fully understand that receiving a *no* means nothing about you as a person, you will likely be sending more and juicier no's in the other direction.

Likewise, juicy yes's are also important to the language of confidence. When you say *yes*, do you do it fully, without qualifications? Do you say *yes* and mean it? Or do you say *yes* when you'd like to say no and then resent it?

Never say *yes* to anything unless you can follow through with energy, excitement and enthusiasm. If you don't, you cheat both yourself and the other person. Refrain from saying *yes* unless you are fully definite about your answer. When you're sure, say *yes* with power and know that your belief in yourself as a confident decision-maker is growing.

Mediocrity

"That'll do."

"It's O.K."

"It's good enough for government work."

"Close enough."

If you want to develop a picture of yourself as average, persist in using the language of mediocrity to program your bio-computer. This type of language will help you create a mindset of yourself as a person who settles for less than you want. It shifts your expectations downward and undermines your confidence.

Confident people don't settle. They have high expectations and develop patterns of language that reflect those expectations.

Attack

Our language is full of attack words.

"You have to *fight* for success."

"Better learn to *fight* for what's yours."

"*Strike back* quickly or they'll really gain on us."

"Let's *wrestle* with that for awhile."

"We've got to *fight* that."

Attack words come primarily from people who feel threatened and who lack confidence. When you tell yourself you must fight for success or fight for what's yours, you're also telling yourself you're not sure you'll get it. If you were confident, if your expectations were high, it would not be necessary to fight and use language that refers to struggle and strain.

Confident people go with the flow. They know that what's theirs will come to them. They don't have to demonstrate strength by proclaiming it loudly with language. Their strength is in their belief in themselves. It's an inner strength that demands no outside verbiage to prop it up.

Summary

Confidence is belief, belief in yourself and in your abilities to handle the situations and circumstances that arise in your life. Belief comes from thought, the thoughts you continuously think about yourself and your abilities. Thoughts are made up of words, words that affirm or deny your talents, characteristics and specialness.

Each of us has the power to choose words that affirm or deny. We can select language that expects the best or the worst. We can structure our talk to reflect fear or faith. In each instance, the choice is ours.

You can begin today to put more confidence in your life by using the language of confidence. Begin with any strategy presented in this chapter. Design an affirmation for yourself. Say "when" instead of "if." Replace hoping and wishing with positive expectation. Eliminate the use of titles, jargon or exaggeration. Say juicy *yes's* and juicy *no's*.

It doesn't matter where you begin. It does matter that you do begin. By taking action on any of the ideas presented here, you activate forces that help you move towards greater confidence.

First of all, your subconscious mind is impressed with actions. By changing your words, you are taking action and acting as if you are confident. When you act as if you are confident, you are more likely to be seen as confident and are more likely to internalize a picture of yourself as confident. Taking the necessary action to change your language is an important first step.

Second, your new language immediately begins to reprogram your bio-computer. As you consistently change your language patterns, you steadily remind yourself of your emerging confidence with new beliefs and expectations. The cumulative effect of a consistent plan to gradually eliminate your insecurity programming by replacing it with language of confidence will accelerate your growth. As you persist in your verbal work, you will find your confidence increasing rapidly.

Do it. Expect it. Appreciate it. And don't be one bit surprised. You're worth it.

Chapter Seven

THE LANGUAGE OF HERE AND NOW

Our culture has produced many catch phrases that remind us of the importance of living in the here and now. "Today is the first day of the rest of your life," "This moment is all there is," and "Now is the only now," are a few of them. These slogans have appeared on wall hangings, calendars, posters and bumper stickers. Yet, for all their popularity, these "live now" sayings have not had much impact on our everyday language. Consider the following:

"I'm *going to* do that eventually."

"*If only* I had warned him about her."

"I *should have* done it more carefully."

"He *ought to* feel guilty about that!"

"*When* I retire, I'm going to catch half the fish in this river."

Each of the sentences above indicates a decision to live in the past or the future. Their use implies an ignoring of the "here and now" reality of our lives. They reveal a surrendering of our present moments and a weakening of our personal power. Let's take a closer look.

Our only point of power is now. For all our good intentions about tomorrow, it is not possible to be powerful tomorrow. Not during this moment. Nor is it possible to be powerful yesterday. Yesterday is already gone.

Regardless of whether we want to lose weight, develop a regular exercise program, or finish a financial report, we can only take action now. It's impossible to take action a second ago or a second from now. We have only one point of power — now.

Language can help or hinder us in our endeavors to live in the present moment. It helps us focus on the dead past, concentrate on the imagined future, or stay centered and attuned to the here and now.

This chapter will detail ways we use language to promote or interfere with present moment living. You will have an opportunity to listen to your own language and discover clues to determine where you are living at any given moment. You will also learn alternatives for language that focuses on yesterday and tomorrow, and develop patterns of speech that encourage you to use your point of power and enjoy the present.

Perhaps you're like Frank, who explained at one of my workshops, "I don't ever seem to be living in the present. When I drive to work in the morning, I'm thinking about what I'll do when I get there. When I get to work, my thoughts are about what I'll say at the luncheon meeting. When I get to the luncheon meeting, I think about what I want to accomplish that afternoon. When the afternoon arrives, my mind is on what I want to do when I get home. When I drive home, I wonder about what we'll be having for dinner. When I eat dinner, I plan what I'll watch on T.V. When I watch T.V., I decide whether or not to snuggle up with my wife that night. The next day this process starts all over."

Frank spends most of his time living in the future. He is, in effect, missing his whole life. His example is extreme, of course, and not unlike what many of us do from time to time. Frank is futuring — spending his present moments thinking about, dwelling on and predicting the future.

FUTURING

How much of your time do you spend living in the future? Your language can serve as a clue. You can use it to determine the degree to which you live in the future or the present.

What If

"What if" is one such clue. You've probably heard yourself say it aloud recently. If not, perhaps you remember saying it silently to yourself.

"What if she says, 'No'?"

"What if it doesn't work?"

"What if the car breaks down?"

"What if I catch a cold?"

"What if" is futuring. It is an example of using words that help you concentrate on the imagined future which may or may not occur. "What if" keeps you from enjoying your present moments by focusing your energy and attention on something that may never happen.

"What if" sentences help you to put negative pictures in your mind. If you say to yourself, "What if she says, 'No'?" you are likely to picture her saying, "No." If you think, "What if the car breaks down?" you are apt to create a picture in your mind of a stalled car.

Once you create negative pictures for yourself, you often respond emotionally and physically as if those imagined scenes were real. If you imagine her saying "No," you are likely to feel the disappointment even though you haven't asked her yet. And since you already feel the disappointment, you're less likely to take action by asking for what you want.

When you hear yourself saying "what if," use that as a reminder that you're living an illusion. Use it as a signal to remind yourself to get back to present moment living.

When you hear your "what if," lessen the impact that language has on you by immediately stating the opposite. If you catch yourself saying, "What if the car breaks down?" follow it with, "What if the car doesn't break down?" When you notice your words are, "What if he gets really mad?" re-mind yourself with, "What if he chooses to be really happy?"

To get more in touch with the significance of "what if," complete the following exercise. Think of some goal you want to accomplish or something you want to do tomorrow. Write out your "want to" on a piece of paper. Underneath it write two or three "what if's" that you could use to prevent yourself from accomplishing your objective.

SOMETHING I WANT TO DO TOMORROW

"I want to run six miles."

WHAT IF'S

What if it rains?

What if I get home late and it's dark outside?

What if I don't feel like it?

Now write a couple of "what if's" that seem preposterous. Think up some that couldn't possibly happen to prevent you from reaching your goal. Write those under your other "what if's."

What if I'm arrested and go to jail?

What if there is an earthquake?

What if I break a leg?

Now re-examine your entire list of "what if's." Realize that none of them is likely to happen. Know that if one does, you are skilled enough to handle the situation as it arises. Now, crumple up your paper and throw it away. When you crumple it, do it with feeling, reminding yourself that your personal power lies in present moment living. Then get on with the task of reaching your goal.

"What If" Variations

Variations of "what if" are "it might" and "it could."

"*It might* rain and spoil our picnic."

"*He might* not like my presentation."

"*It could* be sold by the time we get there."

"*She could* refuse to grant the interview."

It's possible for me to use up my present moments worrying about this book by thinking or saying, "It might not sell," or "It could be a bomb." In terms of this book, the future is unclear. I don't know for sure whether it will sell. I expect it to sell. I believe it will sell. Still, I don't know *for sure*. One thing I do know for sure is that any amount of time I spend worrying or wondering about it is time not spent working on it. If I use up enough present moments futuring, there won't be any book, and I will have created the very situation I wanted to prevent.

Worry

"What if," "it might" and "it could" are signs of worry. And worry is a useless emotion. In fact, it is more than useless. It is immobilizing.

Worry is nothing more than using words to put pictures in your mind of all the terrible things that could happen in the future. It's a form of goal-setting that programs your mind with negatives.

Spending time worrying is a waste of time because most of the things we worry about never occur. Those things we worry about that do happen aren't prevented by worrying anyway. By worrying, we trick ourselves into thinking we're being effective. Actually, we're just filling up our minds and our time with worry and preventing ourselves from doing something constructive.

Don't confuse worry with being concerned. It's possible to be concerned and to care without being worried. Consider the following example.

I have a twenty-two-year-old daughter who is a recovering alcoholic. She lives alone, a thousand miles away from family. Although I love her and care about how she's doing, I don't worry. My mother has a difficult time understanding why I don't worry. She, like many other people in our culture, have caring and concern confused with worry. A recent phone conversation I had with my mother illustrates the point.

"Aren't you worried about Marti?"

"No"

"You aren't?"

"No, I don't worry about her."

"Well, I am. I worry about her all the time. I think you ought to worry about her too."

"Worry doesn't help, Mom. It doesn't do any good. I care about Marti, I think about her, and I don't worry."

"Well, I'll worry about her for the both of us then."

"Why would you want to do that?"

"Well, somebody's got to worry about her."

"It doesn't help, Mom. Do you think worrying helps her to make healthy decisions, attract positive friends or anything else useful? Worry doesn't change anything."

"You might be right, but I wouldn't like it if I didn't worry."

My mother doesn't understand my beliefs about worry. She is busy living out her belief that worry and being a conscientious, caring person are synonymous.

Like my mother, most worriers believe their worry is helping. They believe their worry, which prevents them from being happy in this moment, is making things better for tomorrow. In truth, worrying today not only doesn't help improve tomorrow, it effectively keeps worriers occupied and prevents them from taking any constructive action. I agree with the anonymous quote that says, "Worrying is like rocking in a rocking chair. It gives you something to do, but it doesn't get you anywhere."

An antidote to worry is decision-making. Worry occurs more frequently when there has been no decision made concerning a situation. Because there is no decision, the future is unclear. Once a decision is made, a plan of action emerges. That action plan now gives the worrier something to do. Doing something now helps eliminate worry.

When you become aware that you are worrying, STOP. Ask yourself if there is a decision to be made about the present situation. See if you can find something to do now to alleviate the circumstance you are worrying about. Make a decision. Then follow through and do something. See if that doesn't jar you back to present moment living.

Hoping and Wishing

Hoping and wishing are related to worry. Described in detail in Chapter Six, hoping and wishing are techniques for living in the future.

Hoping and wishing help worriers pass time. These people worry and hope and worry and hope. Time goes by and things remain the same. The tragedy of this cycle is that worriers and hopers actually believe they are using their minds to do something worthwhile. They believe worrying and hoping are useful. They are wrong.

By hoping and wishing, you announce to your subconscious mind that you expect your desires fulfilled sometime in the future. Since your expectations are focused on the future, you are in effect asking for inaction in the present. Ask and you shall receive.

You hope and wish things will be better in the future. And the future never arrives. Because when it does, it's not the future anymore. Since the future never arrives, neither does the manifestation of your desire. And you're left to hope and wish things get better in the future.

Hoping and wishing can also be a way to program yourself to experience pain. By hoping and wishing, you use words to create models in your head of how things should be.

"I hope he gets a decent job."

"I wish I had a new car."

"I wish she would study harder at school."

When you use "hope" and "wish" to create in your head how your world should be and your world doesn't conform to the models you've created, your programming causes you to experience the separating emotions of disappointment, hurt, anger, etc. When your expectations are not met, and your programming has been so strong that you don't let go of those expectations, you cause suffering in yourself. That suffering, which takes the form of unhealthy emotional responses, was created by your hoping and wishing. To continue to hope and wish is to continue to set yourself up for disappointment and more suffering.

Someday Soon

"*One of these days* I'll clean the garage."

"*When* I get my head together, I'll finish that."

"*Eventually,* I'm going to tell her the truth."

"I'm *going to* quit this job if he doesn't straighten up."

Ever hear yourself utter one of the phrases italicized above? If so, you may be suffering from the Someday Soon Syndrome. Someday Soon is a technique for postponing. It signals a decision not to take action and to put off until later. It's another example of futuring.

"I'll do it when" is a classic example of Someday Soon talk. I hear it frequently from friends, relatives and colleagues as well as from myself.

I'll do it when I'm . . .

old enough.

big enough.

brave enough.

tough enough.

I'll do it when I . . .
                graduate.
                finish my master's.
                get my doctorate.
                retire.
I'll do it when . . .
                I get married.
                I have children.
                the kids move out.
                I get my divorce.
                I remarry.
I'll do it when I . . .
                lose ten pounds.
                gain ten pounds.
                buy some new clothes.
                feel like it.

All the examples above refer to when something will be done. Yet, each more loudly refers to when it won't be done, and that is right now.

Frequent use of "I'll do it when" is an indication that you spend a lot of time waiting — waiting until the kids get older, waiting until you get a new job, or waiting until your mother-in-law moves out. You can wait for a long time for your ship to come in. In fact; you can spend your whole life standing in line waiting while you sing variations of "I'll do it when."

"I'll be happy when . . ." is one of those variations.

I'll be happy when . . .
                I graduate.
                I have this baby.
                when the kids grow up.
                when I get my hair done.
                when I get a better job.

There is no end to the possible completions to this sentence. There is also no end to the misery you can create for yourself when you choose this style of language.

"I'll be happy when . . ." helps you to create beliefs that happiness is caused by outside events. If you announce, "I'll be happy when I graduate" often enough, you start to believe that it's graduation that produces happiness. Once you believe happiness comes from graduation, getting your hair done, owning a home or any other event or situation, you diminish your sense of personal power. You effectively limit the possibility of creating happiness for yourself in the present moment.

Speaking and believing "I'll be happy when . . ." strengthens your belief that outside events cause your happiness. Choosing words of this nature keeps you focused on the future and thus powerless in the present. In that way, you give up responsibility for creating happiness in your life right now.

Let's Wait

"Let's wait for the right time."

"Let's wait until he shows some interest."

"Let's wait until we know for sure."

"Let's wait until" is another version of "I'll do it when." Both are phrases of indecision and inertia. Their repeated use will effectively program you for non-action. Non-action is the result of the mental habit of waiting for certainty. And that mental habit begins with words.

When you insist on waiting for certainty, you have effectively paralyzed yourself. It's one more way to fill up your present moments with something other than action. And that something is waiting, waiting while you do nothing.

Eventually

"Eventually" is another word that programs your mind for lethargy and inaction. Its use means you are putting off — postponing until a later time. Because of your programming, that later time seldom arrives.

"I'll share it with him *eventually.*"

"*Eventually* I'll clean up the basement."

Could it be when you say you'll do something eventually that you're afraid to do it now? When you hear yourself say that word, ask, "Is there something I'm afraid of?" See if you can get in touch with your fears. List them. Isolate each specific fear. Then push through each one by doing it now.

Or perhaps the use of "eventually" means you don't believe you can do it now. If so, acknowledge your belief and use words that accurately describe your present situation. Choose language that reminds you where you are now and helps you see the choices you are making in this moment.

"I'm choosing not to share it with him at this time," keeps you focused on now. "I'm not going to clean up the basement right now," describes the present situation and helps you stay tuned to how you're using your only point of power — your now.

"One of these days," "I'll do it when," "I'll be happy when," "Let's wait," and "Eventually" are phrases that signal the Someday Soon Syndrome. Notice those phrases. Hear yourself when you say them and remember you're futuring.

When you hear yourself humming a Someday Soon tune, stop. Remind yourself that one road to present moment living is to "do it now." See if you can't find one activity that you could do now that would help you move closer to your goal. Then do it.

Going To

"Going to" is a phrase often used to describe an intention. "I'm going to lose ten pounds," "I'm going to call her tomorrow," or "I'm going to look for a new job," all announce an intention to do something in the future. Since the future never comes, neither does the new job, the call or the loss of ten pounds.

"Going to" implies procrastination and is the first step in putting something off until later. Its use is another clue that you are living in the future.

"Going to" is indefinite. What does it mean? Does it mean a year, a week, or an hour? Who knows? It could mean forever. There's greater personal power in being definite. You lose power being indefinite. The only thing definite about "going to" is that you're definitely not "going to" right now.

Doing is more powerful than "going to." Use your present moments more effectively by doing or not doing. And eliminate "going to" from your vocabulary.

Should/Ought To

"I *should* clean the house."

"I *ought to* loan him the money."

"I *should* be more consistent in my exercise program."

"Ought to" and "should" represent another route to sabotaging your present moments. They are words you use to future, to create anxiety about what is yet to come.

"Should" and "ought to" are ways of getting after yourself by helping you to feel bad. Their use encourages you to focus on the difference between what exists now and what you feel "should" exist in the future. It's a way to put pressure on yourself and increase anxiety.

One way to reduce the anxiety and pressure that result from using "should" and "ought to" is to change them to "could." "I *should* clean the house," then becomes "I *could* clean the house." "I *should* loan him the money," can be changed to "I *could* loan him the money."

"Should" and "ought to" help you get after yourself because they rate you as a person. "I should study harder," is an evaluation. It is self-judgment.

"Could" is a word that describes the situation. It implies no evaluation. "I could study harder," describes the situation. It tells what is possible in the here and now.

Because "could" describes rather than judges, it makes the choices more visible. When you say, "I should study harder," you focus on yourself and get stuck in the evaluation. When you say, "I could study harder," you focus on the choice and perceive that the degree of study is a decision.

Recognize that "could" is an opportunity to make a decision. There is power inherent in making decisions. State your could. "I could study harder." Then decide. Are you going to study harder or aren't you? Once you decide, then change your words again. Change "could" to "will" or "won't." Your statement then becomes, "I won't study harder," or "I will study harder."

Fear and anxiety decrease once a decision has been made. Your sense of personal power increases. State your "will" or "won't" aloud. Feel your power, experience it. Then follow through. And as Wayne Dyer says, "Stop shoulding on yourself."

Shoulding On Others

Another use of "should" that will weaken your ability to live effectively now is putting "should's" on others.

"She should be on time."

"They shouldn't say those kinds of things."

"He should be more courteous."

When you use "should" concerning others, you create models in your head of how the world "should be." Then when others don't live up to your expectations, you're likely to create emotions of anger, irritation, frustation, etc.

When you believe others should be different, you're not accepting what is in the here and now of your life. You're setting yourself up to experience suffering which takes the form of unhelpful emotional responses.

People are what they are. The world is what it is. If you don't like it and it's in your power to change it, do it. If it's not in your power to change, stop hurting yourself with "should's." Accept what is, at least on an emotional level. Don't spoil your present moments by shoulding on others.

Planning for the Future

Often graduate students ask me, "What about planning for the future? I've got to think about the future some if I'm going to accomplish any planning. What's wrong with that?"

Planning for the future is not living in the future. It is living now. Planning is an example of effectively using your present moments to prepare for the future. Once the planning is complete, present moments are used to implement the plan. That, too, is effective present moment living. Planning or implementing a plan only becomes futuring if you spend your present longing, hoping, wondering, waiting or wishing.

Most of us are unaware of the amount of time and attention we give to futuring. Forecasting terrible things that might happen to us, wishing things were different, worrying about possibilities, wondering what will happen, or predicting what we're "going to" all take incredible amounts of energy. Imagine using all that time and energy for living in the present. What a positive force that energy is when used now.

PASTING

Living in the past by replaying yesterday, regretting past decisions, feeling guilty, resenting or rehashing is another way to give up your personal power by ineffectively using up your present moments. If you're busy living in the past, you're not enjoying the present. Pasting is a way to immobilize yourself by using your only point of power to focus on the dead past and replay what cannot be changed.

To what degree do you live in the past? How many of your present moments are spent reliving what is already over? Your language offers you clues. Consider the "if only" clue.

If Only

"If only" is a key phrase used by people who live in the past. It keeps them attached to the past and ineffective in the present.

"If only I had gone to college."
"If only I hadn't married him."
"If only I had listened to my mother."

"If only" is a primary preventer, a way of procrastinating. "If only the economy were better," prevents you from taking a financial risk. "If only I had someone to help me," keeps you from doing it yourself. "If only I had more time," discourages you from using the time you do have.

If only you had gone to college, things would be better. Are you sure? Things might be worse. Who knows how things would have turned out had you gone to college? No one.

The only thing you know for sure is what is now. You didn't go to college, you did marry him, or you didn't listen to your mother. Why not spend your present moments celebrating what is, what does exist in your life, or deciding what you want to change? Stop programming your mind with the language of the past and use "If only's" as a clue to nudge yourself back into the present.

Regretting and Resenting

"If only" is one of the phrases we use to regret and resent. Others follow:

"I *wish I had* studied harder in school."
"I *would have liked to* have been born to richer parents."
"Why didn't I see how shallow she was?"
"How could I have made that mistake?"

The language of regret keeps your energy zeroed in on opportunities lost. It's a style of speaking and thinking that prevents you from seeing the opportunities that exist now. When you're regretting, you're too busy rehashing the past to live fully in this moment.

Resenting keeps you preoccupied with blaming. It's a way to feel bad about yourself or others for things that have happened in the past. Resenting is the mental refighting of some situation that has already occurred. Using the language of resentment is a no-win situation because there is no way you can change the past. You can only hurt yourself by continuing to use words that program you to hold tightly to what is over.

You give away personal power when you resent and regret. In addition to the power you lose by not using the moment effectively, you also lose power through the way you view yourself.

How can you see yourself as self-reliant if you're busy doing regret? How can you perceive yourself as self-determined if you're thinking and speaking resentment? When you regret and resent, you keep yourself busy looking for external injustice and strengthen your programming that says what happens outside of you (external events) is more important than your inside experience (your interpretation). By resenting and regretting, you focus on others and don't look closely at how you contributed to the situation or how you are keeping it going now with your choice of language.

"If only," "I wish I had," "Why didn't I" and other phrases of regret can be the signal for you to step back into present moment living. When you notice self-talk that keeps you stuck in the past, cut it off. Then ask yourself, "What can I do now that will impact that situation?" When you determine an appropriate action, take it. If you don't identify an action or choose not to take one, at least enjoy the moment you do have. Don't waste your present doing regret and resentment.

Reminiscing

Reminiscing about the good old days is still another way to use language to live in the past.

"We sure had fun when . . ."

"Remember the time . . ."

"Wasn't it wonderful when . . .?"

"We used to . . ."

Reminiscing can be a harmless look back or a harmful desire to relive the past. It all depends on the frequency and intensity of your thoughts.

A few moments of reminding yourself of things you once enjoyed and may choose to recreate again can be a helpful way to use your present. Yet longing to do what you did back when or dwelling on the past for long periods of time is an immobilizer.

Watch out for thoughts of yesterday. They can rob you of your present by draining both time and energy.

"Should Have"/"Ought to Have"

"Should have" and "ought to have" are two more phrases that signal living in the past. They are examples of using up present energy recalling what could have been if you had chosen to act differently.

"I *should have* called my mother this weekend."

"I *shouldn't have* told him off."

"I *should have* studied harder."

"I *ought to have* known better."

It's never possible to redo present moments once they have occurred. Time spent lamenting how you used your previous moments is a waste of time. It keeps you stuck in the past and prevents you from taking corrective action now.

Do not confuse this with learning from the past. Yes, it is useful to spend time, thought and energy looking at past behavior, learning from it, and moving in a new direction. That strategy helps mobilize you for growth and change.

"Should have," though, is an immobilizer. It's a phrase we use to help ourselves feel guilty; a technique we use to get after ourselves.

"But if I don't feel guilty, why would I ever want to change?" I'm asked on some occasions. Usually the question comes from a workshop participant who believes guilt is healthy and that he needs to give himself a swift kick.

Guilt works in the opposite way. Rather than mobilize one for action, it immobilizes. Guilt is nothing more than anger that is directed at yourself. It keeps you feeling separate from yourself and others. While you're busy berating yourself, you're doing nothing in the present to change the situation.

Guilt does not change anything you've done. It doesn't help you to go back and replay it. Nor does it help you to change your present behavior. Any change which occurs after you've experienced guilt occurs in spite of guilt, not because of it.

Also, any time you spend feeling guilty is time not spent seriously looking at who or what it is you are angry about. Choosing anger turned inward (guilt) is a way of giving up your power by letting other people and situations control your reactions to them.

Instead of "should have" use "could have."

"I could have saved more money when I was younger," is kinder than "I should have saved more money."

"I could have been nicer to her," is more descriptive than "I should have been nicer to her."

"I could have told the truth," helps you focus on options. "I should have told the truth," confines and limits.

Take a serious look at your "could have's." Learn from them. Use them to decide what you want now. Then announce it. "I want to tell the truth," "I want to save more money," or "I want to be nicer to her." Saying what you want helps you focus on change and growth. It tells where you are now rather than keeping you stuck in the past.

Learning from mistakes of the past and changing present behavior is personal power in operation. Decide what you want. Then do it.

The Miss Connection

"I sure am missing him."

"I missed you."

"Will you miss me?"

Ever use the style of language above? If you do, it could be another clue that you're not living in the present. Any time you're missing someone, you're occupying your now space with thoughts about the past or wishing for the future. It's an effective way to diminish your present joy.

164

Some people believe missing another person is a sign of love and affection. It isn't. Missing someone only measures the degree to which you choose to give up your present moments for that person. It has nothing to do with love.

On several occasions throughout the year, my wife, Dee, and I go in opposite directions. We have chosen active life styles and each month there are some days when one of us is out of town. On those occasions, we don't miss each other.

Don't misinterpret here. I love Dee very much. I enjoy being with her. We purposefully plan to share time, interests and energy together. Still I don't miss her when she's gone.

If I'm missing Dee, I'm not totally involved in what I'm doing. If I'm wishing she were here, I'm wasting my present moments on the past or future. My goal is to enjoy myself when Dee is gone, and appreciate her when she returns. When I do that, I have more to share with her when we do get together. If I spend my present moments missing her, I won't have as much to share.

I don't want to miss Dee. Nor do I want her to miss me. I want her to enjoy herself when we're separated by focusing her full attention on whatever experiences she's having. I want her to do that because I know that if she does, she'll have more energy, enthusiasm and excitement to plow back into our relationship when we reconnect.

Instead of "I missed you" which announces how you were pasting, choose language that tells the other person how you're feeling *now*.

"Wow, I'm really glad to be with you."

"Seeing you again is fun for me."

"I like the time I spend with you."

Each of the sentences above shares how you're feeling this moment. It helps you to concentrate on what's happening inside you now and to step out of the game which judges love by the amount of present moments you gave up missing the other person.

Complaining

Complaining is a strategy we often use to waste our present moments on something other than direct action. It's easy to complain. There are a lot of situations and events in the world that don't meet our models of how things "should" be.

The state of the economy is in bad shape. My boss doesn't understand me. Gas prices are too high. My cousin is always late. Politicians make the wrong decisions. And the White Sox lose more than I'd like them to.

It's possible to complain about anything. Every person, situation or circumstance in your life is fair game. If you look hard enough, you can find something to complain about.

Recently I complained about some teachers with whom I was working. They had been to one of my workshops and didn't fit my models of how workshop participants should be. I complained about their negative attitude, their lack of humor and their efforts to sabotage my presentation. I complained about their misconceptions, their tardiness and their rude behavior. I even complained about their complaining.

I spent 15 minutes complaining about these teachers. I complained so convincingly, that I got several of my colleagues to agree with me, which widened the circle of complaining.

As I complained, my rational mind continued to feed me proof that I was right. My mind recalled supportive evidence from my workshop and fed it to me right on schedule. It supplied an endless stream of proof which fueled my complaining and helped fan it into an intense heat.

The longer I complained, the more worked up I got. Near the end of the 15 minutes, I was feeling separate from those teachers, alone and angry. And every second I spent focusing on their behavior and attitudes effectively prevented me from concentrating on my own attitude, which is the only one I have any control over anyway.

Later I remembered that I'm only in charge of *my* actions and behavior. Teachers who attend my workshops are in charge of *their* actions and behaviors. Since I only control myself, the wisest use of my time would be to examine what *I* could do differently next time to influence their choices about their behaviors and attitudes.

What do you complain about? Make a list now. List the people, circumstances and events in your life that you tend to grumble over. Now get specific. If you listed Uncle Bill as one of the people you complain about, describe exactly what it is about him that you annoy yourself with. Is it Uncle Bill's preference for telling ethnic jokes, his habit of interrupting you in the middle of a sentence or his style of dress? Take time now to write a specific complaint for each person and situation on your list.

Find a friend to use as a partner for this activity. Call a friend or relative if necessary. Tell them about Uncle Bill. Ask them to complain with you for five minutes. Complain as effectively as you can. Upon conclusion of your five-minute complaint time, write out your feelings. Then answer the question, "Is anything different?" If so, list it.

Now repeat the process with another friend. Only this time engage in five minutes of problem-solving. What exactly is the problem? What can be done to alleviate this situation or change your perception? What activities can you engage in that will help diminish this problem? Focus on you. What can you do to take care of yourself here and now?

Once again, when you finish, write out your feelings. Then answer the question, "Is anything different?" Write your reply.

Now compare your two answers and draw a conclusion. I get more mileage out of problem-solving than I do out of complaining. I feel an increased sense of personal power when I focus on solutions rather than complaints. What about you? Is complaining or problem-solving more useful in your life?

Here and Now

Think of what you would do if you had two weeks to live. Make a list of activities you would engage in, people you would see, and fences you would mend. Are there apologies you would make, appreciations you would share or goals you would accomplish? Are there new foods you'd eat, places you'd see or adventures you'd arrange? How would you spend the two weeks?

Now realize that I didn't say, "What if you had *only* two weeks to live?" I asked, "What would you do if you had two weeks to live?" You do have two weeks to live and probably many more. *Now* is the only time any of us have; perhaps it's the time to begin doing the items you listed.

To become more centered in present moment living, monitor your language. Examine it for phrases that reflect the past and future. Change your words to help you concentrate on living now.

There is power in doing. And more power in doing it now. Live in that state of watchful awareness and give your attention to your current language. The language you used yesterday is gone. Tomorrow's words are not yet here. Pay attention to today's words. Make decisions on those you want to change. Follow through. And do it now.

Chapter Eight

STRATEGIES FOR CHANGE

It is no accident that you are reading this book. You may have been attracted by the title, the cover, or by the suggestion of a friend. As you leafed through it, a word, a phrase, or a chapter heading probably helped build your interest. Chances are you read and continued to read because something in the text spoke to that part of you that was ready to listen.

I assume you have been challenged, perplexed, amused and entertained. I also assume you have come to new understandings and have found messages that hold strong meaning for you. That's a helpful start.

Since you've read this far, I imagine you have developed an appreciation of language as programming and see the connection between words, perception and behavior. My hunch is you've thought about the role words play in how you experience reality, and you are viewing language as a medium of perception as well as a medium of communication. If so, you've strengthened your helpful start.

Any entertainment, enjoyment or learning that has resulted from your connection with this book is important. Any question, challenge or new perception you initiated while reading in this text is also of value. And none of it means a thing unless you go out into the world and do something different.

If you continue to do the behaviors you've always done, you'll continue to get similar results. If you cook a pizza the first time and leave the oven on pre-heat, the top burns and the bottom stays uncooked. If you cook a second pizza and leave the oven on pre-heat, the top burns and the bottom stays uncooked. If you cook a third pizza and leave the oven on pre-heat you know what will happen. That's right, the top burns and the bottom remains uncooked.

Your oven has been on pre-heat long enough. It's time to turn it to bake.

So where do you start? Where's the button for bake? With all the ideas presented in this book it is conceivable that you could overwhelm yourself with possible places to begin.

"How Are You?"

I suggest you begin by changing your response to the often asked question, "How are you?" We all hear that question several times a day as well as variations like, "How ya doing?" and "How's it going?" These questions provide a useful starting place to begin working on your language. They are also an opportunity to remind yourself of the importance of how you choose to talk to yourself and others.

When someone asks, "How are you?" *do not* respond with, "O.K.," "average," "fair to mid'lin," "could be better," "I've been worse," "so-so," "it's too early to tell," "wait 'till I wake up and I'll let you know," or any other variation that programs your bio-computer with a message that is less than ecstatic. If you're currently using one of the phrases above, stop! Remember, language is programming. Get in the habit of responding with words like, "wonderful," "incredible," "superb," "unbeatable," "a notch above excellent," "harmonious" or my favorite, "invincible."

As you respond to these habitual inquiries of others with words that communicate energy and enthusiasm, you will begin to feel more energetic and enthusiastic. You will be using those opportunities to strengthen your newly emerging habit of using words to create your own reality.

By changing how you respond to "How are you?" you take conscious control of your programming. When you take charge of what goes in, you affect what comes out. You become more self-responsible.

Instant Change

Language is one area of our lives where we have the capacity for instant change. We don't need the cooperation of another person, a certain income level or a college education. We can change our language ourselves, regardless of the circumstances that surround us. And we can do it now.

In order to learn new language patterns we must begin by paying attention to the language we do use. We use language so often it is easy to take our typical patterns for granted. We use it without thinking, without consciously making a choice. Many of us have erroneously been taught that language is an act of reporting rather than one of creating. We have learned to give little or no attention to how language structures the way we experience the world. As a result, our language has become loose and often goes unquestioned. It's time to question our language patterns and begin the process of tightening them up.

Our language patterns were learned. To replace the patterns we don't want, it is necessary to learn new language.

Paying Attention

Paying attention comes first. The act of noticing precedes conscious change. Once you notice your thoughts, your words or your actions, you are in a position to do something about them. You are in control. By effectively exercising that control, you can choose your future.

Begin paying attention by cultivating the skill of inner listening. If you're serious about wanting to change your language, paying attention to your self-talk is crucial.

Set some time aside to practice monitoring your headstream. How about the first thing in the morning just after you wake up? Lie there for a few minutes and simply notice your thoughts. Watch them as they go by. Don't judge them or change them. Just let them come and go. Practice noticing.

How do you talk to yourself in the morning? What do you say to yourself? Listen for "have to's" or "can't's." Are your thoughts positive or negative? Get in touch with that constant chatter that goes on between yourself and yourself.

How about when you stand in front of the mirror in the morning as you shave or comb your hair? Use those few moments to listen internally. What are you telling yourself. Don't get caught up in the conversation. Just listen to it and stay conscious of your role as listener.

This may not be easy to do at first. After years of unconscious self-talk, it may take a concerted effort to monitor your thoughts. Persist. Your skill at paying attention to what you are paying attention to will improve with practice. And as you notice what you are conscious of, you enlarge your awareness and become conscious of even more.

When you become more skilled at monitoring your internal dialogue during your designated listening time, practice listening to yourself during non-scheduled times. Do it while driving the car, as you jog, or while standing in line at the grocery store. Or listen to yourself any time you experience strong emotion. If you feel jealous, lonely, frustrated, ecstatic or satisfied, take a minute and listen internally. See if you can hear what you're telling yourself. Become even more aware of how you talk to yourself.

When you become more proficient at hearing what you're telling yourself, turn your ear towards others. What are your friends and co-workers saying with their language? Are they saying things about themselves or others that might be influencing the way you come to perceive the world? To what degree do you buy in to those language patterns.?

Examine closely the words you let influence your life. The news programs you listen to, the magazines you read, even the billboards you notice have an effect. Are you conscious of the messages they are sending?

What kinds of music do you listen to? Pay attention to the lyrics. What messages exist there? Does your choice of music help you program yourself for confidence or doubt? Does it help you feel in or out of control in your life? Are the messages sad and pitiful or happy and positive?

What about television? How is your favorite program programming you? Learn to hear what you watch and watch what you hear. Review your favorite program from a new perspective. Ask yourself, "Are these the kinds of messages I want entering my bio-computer? Is this what I want influencing my beliefs?"

Do you watch the evening news? If you do, you're filling your bio-computer with violence, flood, fire, famine, and theft; you are helping create a disaster consciousness. Strikes, embezzlement, sickness, auto wrecks, murder, kidnapping and other unpleasant events predominate on the evening news. Is the latest catastrophe the last thing you want on your mind before you go to sleep?

You also program your bio-computer by what you choose to read. Yes, programming can come from written as well as spoken words. Many newspapers out-disaster the evening news. Bad news sells. Go through your local paper some time with a red crayon. Put an "O" on every negative story you find. Put a "+" on anything positive. When you get done, look the paper over again quickly noticing the "+'s" and "O's." Ask yourself how much of that material you want stored in your bio-computer.

What about the books and magazines you read? What are the messages you're picking up? Is the author using self-responsible language? Have you looked closely at the messages written on T-shirts? Do you own a bowler's excuse shirt that lists 25 reasons why you don't bowl well or a shirt that says, "I can't believe I ate the whole thing"? Listen to what you wear. Do you have buttons, stickers, or patches that program you in one direction or the other?

Become sensitized to the messages that surround you. Remember, if you're not willing to take charge of your own programming, someone else already is.

Exercise

With awareness comes ripeness for change. When you're consistently hearing your internal dialogue, noticing the language patterns of others and picking up the programming that comes from the media, you're ready to begin a language exercise program.

Yes, exercise. It's important to tone up those language muscles. Not exercising your language is as unhealthy as not exercising you body.

It's time to make a commitment to the process of changing your language. And part of that process involves exercise. I'm talking about vocal workouts, using words and language patterns in specific practice sessions.

Think of your vocal workouts an *innercise*. Just as *exercise* helps keep your exterior in shape, *inner*cise will lead you to inner fitness.

Warm-Ups

Begin with warm-up activities. I don't want you going out into the world cold without first stretching your inner apparatus. Warm-up activities will get you ready for the daily rigors that lie ahead. They will allow you to break into new language patterns gradually with the confidence and ease that comes from being in shape.

Begin your warm-up innercise in the morning. Start by reminding yourself about how you're choosing to feel that morning. "I'm choosing energy" or "I'm choosing to be less than alert" are ways to activate alternatives to "makes me" thinking.

Next, do several repetitions of other alternatives to "makes me" talk. Do 16 or 20 of these. Put in feeling words that you activate occasionally during the day.

"I choose anger."
"I am excited."
"I make me frustrated."
"I 'm boring myself."
"I make me happy."
"I'm choosing satisfaction now."

For your second innercise, practice some self-responsible phrases (Chapter Three). Do three to five repetitions of each sentence stem. This innercise will help you flex your self-responsibility and develop the power to speak in ways that leave you in control.

"I'm choosing _____(put your words here)_____."

to go to work this morning.
to get up a half-hour later than usual.

"I don't like it when _____(your words)_____."

meetings start late.
I find towels on the floor.

"I want _____(your words)_____."

your help.

a new outfit.
"I won't let me _____(your words)_____ "

>take a week off.
>relax during the day.

Another helpful warm-up activity is to exercise the alternatives to "I can't." Using "don't," "won't" and "choose not to" are ways you can build ownership for the choices you make and the priorities you set in your life. This innercise will strengthen your ability to see these issues as choices and allow you to stop programming your mind for limitation.

Do five repetitions of each variation.

"I don't _____(your words here)_____ "

>lose ten pounds.
>play the guitar.

"I won't _____(your words here)_____ "

>quit smoking.
>tell her off.

"I choose not to _____(your words here)_____ "

>climb mountains.
>sing in a choir.

The final morning tune-up will help you develop the strength to stay free of the judgment trap. Stretch your non-evaluative skills by concentrating on specific descriptive phrases.

Examine the day. Do not evaluate it. Describe it. "The sun is shining. It appears bright, clear and crisp." Or, "the rain is falling in a steady drizzle. Gray clouds extend for as far as I can see."

When you have successfully described the day without evaluation, turn your attention to yourself. When you're fully dressed and ready to begin the day, stand in front of a full-length mirror and practice by describing what you see. Remember, no judgments here.

"My tie is straight. My clothes fit. My shoes are shined. My hair is in place. I smell Old Spice aftershave lotion."

Next concentrate on some of your abilities. Describe, don't rate, how you perceive your abilities. Do ten of these unless you experience some pain, in which case ease up and do a few less.

"I persist until I get things done."

"I start tasks right away."

"I keep the house clean and free from clutter."

"I enjoy being around other people."

"I make the time to communicate how I feel."

If you're resisting doing morning warm-up innercises, examine your self-talk. What are you telling yourself? How are you preventing yourself from doing this activity? There are some clues there for you. Listen and you will hear them.

You wouldn't leave the house in the morning without combing your hair, would you? Give your language as much grooming as your hair. Your hair, your teeth and your body all deserve time and energy each morning. So does your language.

Get a morning innercise routine going and stick with it. Your garden doesn't bloom overnight. It requires regular attention before you can harvest the results. The same goes for your language. If you plant words in your mind each morning and fertilize them with practice, then throughout the day you'll get results. Persist and know your verbal garden will bloom.

Cool Down

Of equal importance to morning warm-up innercises are cool-down activities for evening. Runners cool down following a race by walking and stretching. You can apply that same principle to your language practice by walking through a few evening routines and stretching your language skills.

Begin your cool-down period with affirmations. Design two or three positive statements that reflect your desire and ability to alter your language patterns.

"I always notice the words and phrases I want to change."

"My language is becoming increasingly more self-responsible."

"I speak with confidence and conviction."

Repeat each affirmation five times aloud before you go to bed. Or record them on tape and play them as you fall asleep. Re-mind yourself of three goals you will accomplish tomorrow.

"My words will be positive and full of energy."

"I will change my 'shoulds' to 'coulds'."

"I will give myself descriptive feedback three times today."

Use your evening cool-down sessions as a time for reflection. Look back over the day. Scan it quickly in your mind, recalling those times you enjoyed your choice of language. Recognize yourself appreciatively and descriptively for your efforts. Let positive feelings swell up inside of you. Enjoy those positive feelings. Commit to creating more of them tomorrow.

Journals

I suggest that you buy and use a language journal. Use it to keep track of your innercise program and any significant self-talk that occurs during your warm-up or cool-down practice sessions. Your journal will also be valuable when you begin your next strategy for change — self-assignments.

Self-Assignments

Give yourself a language assignment each day. Self-assignment examples include:
- Use descriptive/appreciative praise five times today.
- Pay attention to my feelings, name them, and use language that helps me remember I own my feelings.
  "I'm choosing anger."
  "I'm doing frustration now."
- Three different times I will tell people what I want in an open, direct manner without using "need."
- Use "and" instead of "but" in my weekly report.

Using your journal to record your self-assignments encourages you to become specific. Specific assignments help you focus your efforts and concentrate on one or two language lessons that have meaning for you. By concentrating on one or two, you eliminate the diluting effect of trying to do everything at once.

Self-assignments can take the form of goals or contracts. By recording your goals or contracts in your journal you have a way of measuring your progress and determining whether or not you are satisfied with it.

Goal-setting leads to goal-achievement. That achievement can be used to foster positive self-talk about your progress. Positive self-talk creates positive feelings. And those positive feelings can serve as the impetus for newer and larger goals.

Journals are an ideal place to record your successes. They help you focus on your successes and help you keep moving in a positive direction.

Rewards

Goal or contract completion is an appropriate time to reward yourself. Rewards can take the form of a pat on the back, a few kind words, an elaborate dinner or a shopping spree.

One way to recognize your own accomplishments is to reward yourself verbally for completing goals or for using helpful words in appropriate situations. Say them aloud or record them in your journal.

"Now, that's the way I want to talk."

"That's more like it."

"Nice going, Chick."

Other possible rewards include having dinner with a friend, buying new shoes or giving yourself a half-hour bubble bath. Reward yourself for change, growth and effort. You deserve it.

After you've accomplished several goals and completed many self-assignments, reading through your journal can be a reward in itself. Read slowly. Enjoy the written record of your wins. Savor them. Get in touch with how far you've come. Feel positive about your progress. Revel in your accomplishments.

Learning From Mistakes

Journals can also be used to record language you hear yourself saying that you want to change.

It would be nice if you could make a decision to change your language and then follow through totally without error. Chances are that won't happen.

It's more likely that you'll be imperfect in your efforts to speak the way you'd like to. Success comes to those who make mistakes, notice and correct them consistently.

Journals will help you be consistent about your corrections. When you notice a phrase or word you wish you'd said differently, record it in your journal. Then underneath it, write two other ways you could have said that phrase. Then say the new phrase aloud.

Practice

Persistent practice is the secret to language development. You can learn to be non-judgmental through practice. You can learn to nurture yourself with practice. And you can use affirmations to create what you want in your life through practice.

Repetition and exaggeration is a form of practice that will increase your chances of success. When you're working with "don't," "won't" and "choose not to" as replacements for "can't," exaggerate them. Over-accentuate the "choose not to" when you use it in a sentence. And say it two or three times more often than necessary.

When you're working on changing "if" to "when," go out of your way to find times to use it. Say, "*When* I get that new job," to seven or eight people within a two-hour period. Say it to yourself five more times.

Remember, your bio-computer responds to repetition. Say it once and your words make an impression. Say it 20 times and the impression is deeper.

Mistakes

Mistakes in oral language can be quickly corrected. There's no paper to erase, no equipment to be repaired and no project to redo.

When you hear a phrase you wish you hadn't said, change your words. Make an instantaneous correction. Say it over the way you want it to sound.

Any time you lose control (or choose to be out of control) you can regain control with self-talk. You never lose your ability to change your mind and your actions with self-talk. You only lose your belief in your ability.

When you hear yourself using words you don't want to use, internally shout, "STOP!" Then envision a giant chalkboard with the word or phrase written on it. Use your imagination and see yourself actually erasing the word in your mind. Then say it over to yourself in a way that is consistent with your new language programming.

The chalkboard strategy is an example of using visualization to improve your language. The balloon technique that follows is another.

Find a quiet, restful place. Use your favorite relaxing technique to quiet your mind and relax your muscles. When you are ready, imagine the word or phrase you wish to eliminate written on a colorful helium balloon. Read it silently to yourself as you turn the balloon slowly in your hands. Say goodbye to the phrase as you let go of the balloon. Watch the phrase rise slowly into the air. See the words getting smaller and smaller. When the balloon has risen so high that the words fade, smile appreciatively to yourself. Watch it turn into a tiny speck and then disappear totally from your sight.

A similar visualization is the airplane skywriter method. Go through all the preliminary relaxing steps and then imagine a skywriting plane on the horizon. Watch as it gets closer and closer. When it is overhead, notice that it spells the phrase you wish to eliminate from your language patterns.

Sit for a moment and watch your phrase float silently in the sky. Pay close attention as a gentle wind carries the words off and out of sight. Enjoy the quiet, peaceful sky that is now free of that phrase forever. Enjoy the moment.

Sometimes a symbolic gesture can help you remove language from your consciousness. Burying or burning words can be just the symbolic gesture to do the trick.

I watched one fourth-grade teacher use the burial method to help her students eliminate "can't" from their vocabulary. She asked her students to fill an entire notebook page full of "I can't's." The children had no trouble with this. They wrote, "I can't do long division," "I can't spell well," "I can't catch very good," "I can't stay up past ten o'clock," and other variations. She did the assignment too.

When all the papers were filled, students folded them in half and deposited them in a shoe box which the teacher had on her desk. When the cover was taped on, the class marched to the far end of the playground. At that point, they dug a hole, placed the shoe box inside and covered it with dirt. They had buried their "I can't's."

After the reading of a eulogy, this teacher marched her students back into class and held a wake. Popcorn and Kool-Aid were distributed and they celebrated the passing of "I can't."

I suspect few, if any, of those students will forget that experience. At the very least they come away from that activity knowing how strongly their teacher felt about "I can't" and language that limits.

What words and phrases do you care about so deeply that you'd be willing to bury them? Or would a burn barrel serve your purposes better?

A junior high teacher I worked with once got so sick of hearing kids put each other down, that he had them write on slips of paper all the put-downs they could think of. Then they took their slips and put them in a barrel behind the school. This teacher torched the slips as the students stood in a circle surrounding the barrel. They all joined hands as their put-downs went up in smoke.

Talk As If

Talk the way you want to sound and you'll alter your language and your behavior. If you're not feeling confident and you want to be confident, use confident words anyway. Talk as if you're confident.

Talk as if you expect the best. Talk as if you believe you can. Talk as if you like yourself. Even if you don't — yet.

Related to "talking as if" is "acting as if." Your bio-computer is also impressed with actions. Add "acting as if" you're confident to "talking as if" you're confident and you've strengthened your confidence programming. Add "acting as if" you believe in yourself to "talking as if" you believe in yourself and you strengthen your programming in that area.

Acting and talking as if can be an unbeatable combination. One strengthens the other. Put them together and watch the positive effects that result in your life.

Do It Now

When you hear a word or phrase you wish you hadn't said, change it. And do it now. Don't say you'll remember next time. Get in the habit of effectively using your only moment of power — now.

Every time you have an opportunity to act and don't, you weaken your programming that says language is an important issue for you. By not following through and changing the language you don't like, you tell yourself it isn't all that important. If you don't respond often enough with necessary language improvements, your bio-computer will stop sending you signals to change.

Don't wait when you receive that message to change your language. Do it now.

"Trying" Doesn't Work

Don't catch yourself in the *trying* trap. Trying doesn't work. Doing does. Anyone busy trying is not busy doing.

Don't *try* to eliminate "only/just" from your vocabulary. Eliminate it by purposefully rephrasing sentences so as not to include it. Don't *try* to refrain from self-criticism. Refrain, by giving yourself descriptive feedback instead. Don't *try* to develop a habit of saying affirmations each morning. Either say them or don't. And don't *try*.

Support

Choose to be around people who use language you like. Being in their presence will heighten your awareness of language. And their words will help program your bio-computer.

If you want to learn about health, choose healthy friends. If you want to grow spiritually, choose spiritual friends. And if you want to develop more self-responsible language, choose friends who use self-responsible language.

Don't leave the act of making friends to chance. Refuse to surround yourself with people who speak of lack and limitation, fear and doubt, judgment and criticism. Reach out to new people if necessary. Actively seek friends whose words and thoughts are positive.

Choosing positive friends is especially helpful when you begin using the concepts presented in this book. Having doubters around you when you are first learning this material adds a negative influence at a critical moment. Doubters and people who mock your efforts at using new language patterns can adversely affect your programming when you are not totally sure of it yourself. Until your belief in yourself and your new style of language grows strong, steer clear of those people who could influence it by expressing doubt.

If you encounter doubters, make sure *your* thoughts dominate. Even with your best efforts to select support people wisely, there will be times when you'll find yourself around relatives, co-workers, neighbors or others who express negative reactions to your choice of language. When those situations occur, double your efforts to monitor your self-talk. Concentrate on telling yourself that your beliefs about language are true for you and work for you. If possible, say silent affirmations to yourself to reaffirm your belief in yourself and in your language system.

When you find people you can count on for support, use them as perception checks. Ask for their help in monitoring your language. Give special requests to special friends. Ask them to listen for "can't's" or "makes me" or other phrases you want to eliminate from your language. Ask them for their honest feedback on the kind of praise you give. Or just talk with them from time to time about how they hear you speaking. Use their perception of your language to check yourself, to gain information about how you're coming across to others.

One way to test a friend's support potential is to let them read your copy of this book. Your mutual discussion of the concepts presented here will help you see where they stand on these issues. This could be the beginning of your support network.

When you do find people who understand your way of speaking, form a support group. Meet regularly to discuss your language experiences. Help each other. The encouragement and feedback you get will accelerate both your individual and collective growth.

Post Your Programming

Another useful strategy when changing your language patterns is to post your programming. Put it on display. Hang up posters, sayings, bumper stickers or reminder cards. "Response-ability" makes a nice bumper sticker to fasten on your refrigerator when you're choosing to put more choice into your language. "Nothing Is Too Anything" is a useful phrase to paste on the bottom of your mirror when you're making an attempt to eliminate "too" from your phraseology. "Faith or Fear?" can be stuck to the dashboard of your car when you're monitoring your thoughts to learn if they communicate fear or faith.

Hang them, tape them, staple or tack them. Use your office, living room, truck or desk drawer. Keep the language you want to use as programming in front of you. Keep it on display, where you can see it often. Use this technique to help sink these concepts into your consciousness.

Steps to Skill Acquisition

Whether you're learning new language skills or any other new skill, it's helpful to keep in mind that skill acquisition follows sequential stages.

The first stage is "Unconsciously Unskillful." In this stage, not only are you unskillful, you don't even know you're unskillful.

When you read a book such as this, take a training or talk with people who share their language knowledge, you gain awareness. You begin to realize that you are unskillful. At that point, you are in Stage II, "Consciously Unskillful."

During the move from Stage II to Stage III you purposefully alter your language patterns and experiment with new words and phrases. During this crossover time, your new language may seem awkward or phony.

Don't be surprised. Feelings of phoniness arise because of your exaggeration of the new language which is necessary for you to learn it. The sense of awkwardness stems from the newness. Your new language patterns are not yet habit.

When your new language sounds phony or awkward to you, rejoice. That is a signal that you are crossing the bridge between Stage II and III.

Stage III is "Consciously Skillful." When you reach that stage, you are skilled with your new language when you consciously think about it. When you intentionally make the effort, your language skills are precise.

When you work at being consciously skillful consistently and often, you will move up to a new plateau. You will reach Stage IV, "Unconsciously Competent." At Stage IV you don't even think about your language. You simply speak with self-responsible, confident, self-affirming language out of habit. You are now so skilled that your use of language becomes unconscious.

To help yourself move consistently through the four stages, nurture yourself with positive self-talk at each stage. For instance, when you catch yourself using a phrase you were attempting to eliminate, don't get after yourself. Give yourself appreciative recognition for noticing. See your noticing as a measure of success. There was a time in your life when you wouldn't have noticed. Congratulate yourself for noticing. Celebrate it and move on towards even greater successes.

Rehearsal

Rehearsing ahead of time is another useful strategy to help you learn the skills contained on these pages. If you know you're going into a situation where you've activated "makes me" language in the past, prepare ahead of time in your mind. Rehearse in your head or aloud with a friend. Hear yourself saying the words you want to be saying later in the real situation.

When you rehearse, go over the situation. Choose your reactions and feel the positive feelings that result from successfully using the words you wish to use.

In important situations it can be helpful to role-play the drama before you actually get into it. Ask a friend to take the role of the other person. Prime them by explaining how that person typically reacts and the language she typically uses. Then have your friend play the role while you play yourself using appropriate language. Debrief when you finish by discussing with your friend how it went. Concentrate on your words, your feelings and the self-talk you used during the role play. Ask your friend for her reactions.

Positive Picturing

When you're learning new language patterns and doing new behaviors, one strategy that can strengthen your learning and doing is positive picturing. Mental rehearsal, as it is sometimes called, is a technique in visualizing. It is using the imagination to picture the positive process and outcome of an upcoming activity. It's a mental run-through of the pending performance.

Positive picturing is another way to program your bio-computer and it is as effective as programming with language.

Our brains are divided into two hemispheres. The left side is the logical, rational, linear, verbal part of our brain. It deals mainly in words. That is the side of the brain you program with language.

The right side of our brain is the part that is intuitive, imaginative and holistic. It deals in pictures and is programmed through imagination.

To get maximum effect from the concepts presented here, it is necessary to use both language and pictures to program your bio-computer. Spend time each day picturing your positive performance using your new language skills. Begin by quieting yourself. Relax by concentrating on your breathing and feeling your muscles getting heavier and heavier. Start with your feet. Tense them and relax them. Tense them and relax them again, telling your feet to relax as you go. Work your way up your legs, over your hips and on through your neck and face, stopping to relax each muscle group as you go.

When you are completely relaxed, take three minutes to do positive picturing. Use your imagination to actually picture yourself successfully using the language. Watch and listen to yourself as you use the language patterns you desire. Notice your reactions in the drama unfolding before you and the reactions of people around you. Imagine their reactions as positive. If you see a negative result, simply put your imagination on rewind. Back up a few spaces and re-run it. Create the outcome exactly as you'd like it to be.

Feel strong emotion as you do this mental rehearsal. Be happy with yourself. Feel confident, proud and successful. Notice the happy feelings of others.

When you've experienced the positive pictures for three minutes, stop. End the session and do what ever is next on your agenda. Trust that your mental practice will help you grow in your efforts to learn and speak new language. It will.

Teach It

Teaching the concepts presented in this book will help you learn them. I write about, give presentations and teach university classes with this material because I want to become more consistent using it myself. The more I teach these notions, the better I learn them.

I first recognized the positive relationship between teaching and learning when I taught fifth graders how to divide fractions. I spent one hour teaching. During that 60-minute period, I presented the lesson, answered questions, demonstrated, and re-presented the lesson. At the end of that 60-minute time period one person had learned how to divide fractions. Me.

Fifteen years prior to that I learned to divide fractions for the first time. I was in fifth grade. Within days I forgot how to do it. I again learned to divide fractions in junior high school. And I forgot again. I learned the same material in high school and again in college while I was taking a course on teaching elementary school math. And each time, I forgot.

I didn't really learn how to divide fractions until I taught the process to ten-year-old students. Organizing the information in my head, rehearsing it silently to myself, hearing it aloud as I explained it to the students, and responding to questions served to help me finally learn how to divide fractions.

When you teach one of these concepts to a friend or neighbor, you'll go through the same process. Organizing the information and rehearsing it in your head will help you learn it. Stating it aloud and hearing it at the same time will give you feedback as to how well you really know it. And responding to concerns and questions will further sharpen your knowledge base.

Danger

Warning! Some people don't want you to teach them how to talk sense. Some people don't want anyone to teach them how to talk sense. Especially you.

There are probably some people in your life who get excited about the things you get excited about. You share new books, ideas and concepts with them often. Generally you agree with these people and enjoy communicating together. The odds are in your favor that one of these people will sit still long enough for you to get in valuable practice time teaching these concepts. Find that person and put her to use listening. And keep in mind throughout the process of teaching that the person you're really teaching is *you*.

There is probably another group of people in your life who, when you think of them in connection with talking sense, you think "they need it." These are people you thought of often as you read the preceding pages and wished they would apply some of these concepts in their lives. These people may include your spouse, children, co-workers, relatives, or neighbors. These people are *not* prime candidates to become your students.

The problem with teaching this material to people who *you* think need it is that *they* don't think they need it. And in most cases they don't want it. Some may even resent it.

If you're serious about wanting significant people in your life to learn to talk sense to themselves, concentrate on yourself. You are the only person who is totally under your control. You are in charge of you. And the only permission you need for growth or risk or change is your own.

Learn these concepts yourself and put them to use in your own life. Model these notions and the important people in your life may notice.

"Attitudes are more easily caught than taught," is a quote I heard somewhere. It can be used to explain the passing of these language ideas from one person to another. Some people, who may not desire to take on the concepts directly from you, can be influenced by just being around you. If you stop trying to teach them, they just might learn it themselves from your example.

Coersion

Coersion doesn't work. It is an effort to control another person. If you're serious about learning self-responsible language and developing self-responsible behaviors, keep this thought in mind. You cannot be self-responsible until you no longer desire to control others. Giving others freedom frees you. Let others choose what's best for them. You decide what's best for you and concentrate on that.

Put your effort into changing your own language patterns rather than into changing others. That will help you reach your goals and may even be caught by someone else.

Speak For Yourself

Recently my mother telephoned and wanted to chat. Her call coincided with a serious family discussion I was having with my oldest son. I told her I was busy and would call her back later. I could tell from the tone of her voice that she didn't like being put off until later.

When the family discussion ended I telephoned my mother. She immediately launched into a full-scale attack about how she didn't like being told to wait and informed me that I had "made her mad." During the course of sharing her feelings, she used several variations of "makes me" phraseology. I was smart enough to realize that this was not an appropriate time to give her a language lesson.

When my mom took a breath, I jumped in and said, "I sure don't like to see *you working yourself up* like this." Later in the conversation I made remarks like, "*You* really *chose to get mad* about this, didn't *you?*" and "I wish *you* wouldn't *hurt yourself* over this issue."

Each time I spoke I used language that communicated that I knew my mother was her own boss, that I knew she was in charge of her own emotions. I didn't use that language to teach her a lesson. I didn't even say it so she would hear it. I said it so *I* would hear it. I did it to help me keep straight in my head that I'm not the cause of my mother's feelings, that I'm not responsible for whether or not she gets mad.

If my mother hears some of my self-responsible language and learns from it, fine. That's a bonus. If she asks me why I use that language and wants to hear my explanation, fine. That's another bonus. Still, I don't say it because I want her to hear it. I say it because I want me to hear it.

When your spouse says, "You really make me mad," you don't have to use that opportunity to preach what you believe about language. Just be there and listen to the feelings. Then tell her what you heard by paraphrasing her words into your language. "Sounds like you're feeling angry," or "You're choosing to be really frustrated," or "You're really getting upset," is appropriate.

Restraint is important here because some people choose to be even more upset when they hear you using self-responsible language. It's helpful with these people to simply change their sentences in your head rather than aloud. Learn to hear their messages the way you want to hear them.

If your boss remarks, "You frustrate me," it may not serve your purposes to reply, "So you're choosing to be frustrated by me," or "I'm sorry you're choosing frustration." Instead, do an inner translation and hear her words in your language.

You can develop the ability to hear the words of others through your language system. When someone says, "You're embarrassing me," you can hear that the person is choosing to be embarrassed. If your child remarks, "You hurt my feelings," you can hear that the youngster is choosing to feel hurt. When a friend informs you, "That depressed me," you can hear that he is depressing himself. When you translate the words of others into your language, you are less likely to choose impatience with them. You are more likely to hear beyond their words to what they are really saying.

You will find, especially at first, that not many people use self-responsible language. We're living in a world that promotes language of denial, judgment, limitation, fear and doubt. It's important that you learn to communicate both ways. If you insist on communicating your way and continually correct those who don't, you'll limit your ability to communicate.

Stay flexible in your language patterns. Flexibility may not get you the exact response you desire. And then it may. Regardless, the person with the most flexibility in any relationship is the one with the greatest possible influence.

Get Started

If you want to make sure something gets finished, *start* it. If learning new language is important to you, *start* learning it. What will be your start? Will you share this book with a friend, buy a journal, or record affirmations to play to yourself as you fall asleep? Will you burn a page of judgmental language, bury your "I can't's" or start a morning innercise program?

Have you made your start? If you haven't, listen to your self-talk. What are you saying to yourself to prevent you from beginning? Are you talking sense to yourself?

190

One Last Word

You can choose your future.

The techniques and concepts presented in this book can help you change your life. Speaking in new ways will help you detach yourself from old habits. New words will lead to a new mind. A new mind will lead to new perceptions. New ways of seeing will lead to new behaviors.

What kind of personality would you choose if you were starting over? Understand that you are starting over. We all do, every day.

What abilities, characteristics, and attitudes would you choose for yourself? Understand that you are choosing.

Your mind is the delivery system for creating your reality. Your language patterns program your mind. Your words are that important.

Speak to produce a desired result. Use language to create what you want in your life. Use words to enhance your personal power. Talk sense to yourself. You're worth it.

BIBLIOGRAPHY

Although most of the material in this book comes from my own experience and personal contact with others, I have found the following resources to be helpful. I list them here for your consideration as support and possible extension to the concepts presented in this text.

BACH, RICHARD. *Illusions: The Adventures of a Reluctant Messiah.* New York, NY: Delacorte Press, 1977.

BALLARD, JIM. *Why Not? How to be Doing What You'd Like to be Doing and Getting Paid For It.* Amherst, MA: Mandala Press, 1976.

BESANT, ANNIE. *Thought Power.* Wheaton, IL: The Theosophical Publishing House, 1979.

BRIGGS, DOROTHY CORKILLE. *Celebrate Yourself: Making Life Work For You.* New York, NY: Doubleday & Company, Inc., 1977.

DISHON, DEE and PATRICIA WILSON O'LEARY. *A Guidebook For Cooperative Learning.* Holmes Beach, FL: Learning Publications, 1984.

DYER, WAYNE. *Gifts From Eykis.* New York, NY: Simon and Schuster, 1983.

_____. *Pulling Your Own Strings.* New York, NY: Thomas Y. Crowell Co., 1978.

_____. *The Sky's The Limit.* New York, NY: Simon and Schuster, 1980.

_____. *Your Erroneous Zones.* New York, NY: Avon Books, 1977.

EMERY, GARY. *A New Beginning: How to Change Your Life Through Cognitive Therapy.* New York, NY: Simon & Schuster, 1981.

EMERY, STEWART with NEAL RAGIN. *The Owner's Manual For Your Life.* Garden City, NY: Doubleday & Co., Inc., 1982.

FABER, ADELE and ELAINE MAZLISH. *How to Talk So Kids Will Listen and Listen So Kids Will Talk.* New York, NY: Rawson, Wade Publishers, Inc., 1980.

FERGUSON, MARILYN. *The Acquarian Conspiracy.* Los Angeles, CA: J.P. Tarcher Co., Inc., 1980.

FETTIG, ART. *The Three Robots.* Battle Creek, MI: Growth Unlimited, 1981.

GALLWEY, TIMOTHY and BOB KRIEGEL. *Inner Skiing.* New York, NY: Random House, 1977.

GAWAIN, SHAKTI. *Creative Visualization.* New York, NY: Bantam Books, 1982.

GILLIES, JERRY. *Money-Love.* New York, NY: Warner Books, 1978.

_____. *Psychological Immortality: Using Your Mind to Extend Your Life.* New York, NY: Richard Marek Publishers, 1981.

GINOTT, HAIM. *Teacher and Child.* New York, NY: The Macmillan Company, 1972.

GLASSER, WILLIAM. *Take Effective Control of Your Life.* New York, NY: Harper and Row Publishers, 1985.

HILL, NAPOLEON. *Think and Grow Rich.* New York, NY: Fawcett Crest, 1960.

HILL NAPOLEON and W. CLEMENT STONE. *Success Through A Positive Mental Attitude.* New York, NY: Pocket Books, 1977.

JAMPOLSKY, GERALD G. *Love Is Letting Go of Fear.* Toronto, Canada: Bantam Books, 1970.

KEYES, KEN, JR. *Handbook to Higher Consciousness.* Marina del Ray, CA: Living Love Publications, DeVorss and Company, 1972

_____. *How To Enjoy Your Life In Spite Of It All.* Marina del Ray, CA: Living Love Publications, DeVorss and Co., 1980.

_____. *Prescriptions For Happiness.* Marina del Ray, CA: Living Love Publications, DeVorss and Company.

_____. *Taming Your Mind.* St. Mary, KY: Living Love Publications, 1975.

_____. *The Hundredth Monkey.* Coos Bay, OR: Vision Books, 1982.

LEBOEUF, MICHAEL. *Imagineering: How to Profit from Your Creative Powers.* New York, NY: McGraw-Hill Book Co., 1980.

MACLEOD, WILLIAM M. and GAEL S. MACLEOD. *Mind Qver Weight.* Englewood Cliffs, NJ: Prentice-Hall, Inc., 1981.

MALTZ, MAXWELL. *Psychocybernetics.* New York, NY: Pocket Books, 1960.

MCKAY, MATTHEW and MARTHA DAVIS and PATRICK FANING. *Thoughts and Feelings: The Art of Cognitive Stress Intervention.* Richmond, CA: New Harbinger Pub., 1981.

MOORMAN, CHICK and DEE DISHON. *Our Classroom: We Can Learn Together.* Englewood Cliffs, NJ: Prentice-Hall, Inc., 1983.

MURPHY, JOSEPH, DR. *Power of the Subconscious.* New York, NY: Prentice-Hall, Inc., 1974.

_____. *The Cosmic Power Within You.* West Nyack, NY: Parker Publishing Co., Inc., 1968.

_____. *Your Infinite Power To Be Rich.* West Nyack, NY: Parker Publishing Co., Inc., 1966.

ORR, LEONARD and SONDRA RAY. *Rebirthing in The New Age.* Millbroe, CA: Celestial Arts, 1977.

OSTRANDER, SHEILA and LYNN SCHROEDER. *Superlearning.* New York, NY: Delacorte Press, 1979.

PEALE, NORMAN VINCENT. *Positive Imaging: The Powerful Way to Change Your Life.* Tappon, NJ: Fleming H. Revell Co., 1982.

REID, CLYDE. *Celebrate the Temporary.* New York, NY: Harper and Row, 1972.

ROSS, RUTH. *Prospering Woman.* Mill Valley, CA: Whatever Publishing Co., 1982

SHINN, FLORENCE SCOVEL. *The Game Of Life and How To Play It.* Marina del Ray, CA: DeVorss and Co., 1925.

STRAUCH, RALPH. *The Reality Illusion.* Wheaton, IL: Theosophical Publishing House, 1983.

STEADMAN, ALICE. *Who's The Matter With Me?* DeVorss and Co., 1966.

SWEETLAND, BEN. *I Can.* North Hollywood, CA: Wilshire Book Co., 1972.

TEUTSCH, JOEL MORIE and CHAMPION K. TEUTSCH. *From Here to Greater Happiness Or How To Change Your Life For Good.* Los Angeles, CA: Price/Stern/Sloan Publishers, Inc., 1959.

TIMMERMANN, TIM and DIANE BLECHA. *Modern Stress: The Needless Killer.* Dubuque, IA: Kendall Hunt Publishing Co., 1982.

TRAININGS AND WORKSHOPS

Professional training on the concepts presented in this book is available through the Institute For Personal Power. Make inquiries to: The Institute For Personal Power, P.O. Box 68, Portage, MI, 49081, (616)327-2761.

Training options include:

Keynote Addresses

"Talk Sense To Yourself"

This 40- to 90-minute presentation is a humor-filled overview of the concepts presented in this book. Thought-provoking and entertaining.

One-Day Training

This presentation covers the basics of talking sense to yourself while giving participants an opportunity to go in-depth on selected concepts.

Lecture bursts, discussion and small group activities are the delivery system for increasing participants' awareness and skills.

In-Depth Training

Three- to five-day in-depth, skill-oriented trainings are also available. Material from each chapter of *Talk Sense To Yourself* is covered as participants have opportunities to practice the material and learn specific skills.

For information on these or other trainings offered by the Institute For Personal Power write:

Institute For Personal Power
P.O. Box 68
Portage, MI 49081
(616)327-2761

OTHER BOOKS AND TAPES
OFFERED THROUGH THE
INSTITUTE FOR PERSONAL POWER

OUR CLASSROOM: WE CAN LEARN TOGETHER
by Chick Moorman and Dee Dishon
$6.95 paperback/$14.95 hard cover (add 10% postage)

This book is designed to help K-6 teachers create a classroom environment where discipline problems are less likely to occur, and where students are less likely to activate the new three R's — Resistance, Reluctance and Resentment. It shows teachers how to build an atmosphere of togetherness and cooperation, and focuses on activities and strategies that foster notions of belonging, interdependence and mutual respect. This text is full of classroom-tested ideas designed to help students see themselves as able, capable and responsible. This book will help you create the "Our Classroom" feeling in your classroom.

A GUIDEBOOK FOR COOPERATIVE LEARNING:
A TECHNIQUE FOR CREATING MORE
EFFECTIVE SCHOOLS
by Dee Dishon and Patricia Wilson O'Leary
paperback ($19.00 pre-paid; $21.00 purchase order)

This guidebook helps classroom teachers enhance their students' achievement through the implementation of cooperative learning activities. Research shows that cooperative methods of instruction and learning develop peer support, provide high motivation, increase on-task time, elicit higher achievement, foster positive attitudes, and facilitate a desirable school climate. The procedures outlined in this book are appropriatè for all levels and content areas — from preschool through graduate school. This guidebook helps educators teach students how to work productively and enjoyably in groups while achieving academic goals. Students who work in classrooms where cooperative groups are used learn to care about others. They learn not only to tolerate individual differences, but to value them as well. Acquisition of the important social skills which are learned in cooperative groups has far-reaching implications beyond the classroom to the school, home and community as students carry these skills into their daily lives.

THE THREE ROBOTS
by Art Fettig
$4.00 paperback/$8.95 with cassette (add 10%postage)
Ages 4-12

This book helps children put the concept of programming your own mind to use in their lives. It is a story about three robots, Pos, Semi-pos, and Neg, who have each been programmed to activate different attitudes. Pos, who has learned to program herself to be happy and positive, helps the other two robots learn the secrets of healthy programming. She teaches them how to feed positive thoughts into their minds to produce positive attitudes and behaviors.

What the robots learned, your children can learn too. Let *The Three Robots* show you the way.

THE THREE ROBOTS AND THE SANDSTORM
by Art Fettig
$4.00 paperback/$8.95 with cassette (add 10% postage)
Ages 4-12

This is the second in a series of books about the three robots, Pos, Semi-pos, and Neg. In this children's book, the robots encounter a roaring, frightening sandstorm. One robot loses a leg, one loses an arm and one gets sand stuck in his joints.

This is a story about disabilities and cooperation. The robots learn how proper attitude and working together are necessary to overcome handicaps and live a joyful, happy life.

STRATEGIES FOR WINNING TEACHING
with Chick Moorman
Two cassette tapes and binder
$15.95/tapes and binder (postage included)

This cassette-tape program delivers practical, proven strategies for winning teaching. Packed with energy, motivation and power, this 75-minute program is a lesson in the power of belief. You can use it to:

- become more powerful and experience more enjoyment of your professional practice
- help students learn to believe in themselves
- re-vitalize, re-energize, and re-inspire yourself, your students, or your staff

Learn to get the Force working with you by:

- employing the doughnut theory and always expecting the best
- sharing yourself with students
- concentrating on "I Can-ness"
- becoming solution-oriented
- activating the success cycle for you and your students

All of the materials described in this section may be ordered through The Institute For Personal Power, P.O. Box 68, Portage, MI, 49081, (616)327-2761.

About The Author

Chick Moorman, M.A., is the Co-Director of the Institute For Personal Power, a consulting firm designed to enhance individual and organizational effectiveness. He is a former classroom teacher, and has been a workshop leader, training facilitator and keynote speaker since 1971. He also teaches graduate classes for Michigan State University.

Chick Moorman has done consultation and contractual work for school districts, parent groups, and business and industry. Chick's versatility has been documented by his consistent high ratings by participants whether he is giving a keynote address or facilitating an in-depth training. He is an active member of the National Speakers' Association and The Professional Speakers' Association of Michigan.

Mr. Moorman received his B.A. and M.A. degrees from Western Michigan University in the field of education. He is the co-author of *Our Classroom: We Can Learn Together,* Prentice-Hall, 1983.